India's Act East Policy

India's Act East Policy

Edited by

Josukutty C.A.

Associate Professor and Honorary Director,
Survey Research Centre, Department of Political Science,
University of Kerala, Thiruvananthapuram

New Century Publications
New Delhi, India

NEW CENTURY PUBLICATIONS
4852 / 24, 1st Floor,
Ansari Road, Daryaganj,
New Delhi – 110 002 (India)

Tel.: 011-4101 7798; 4358 7398; 98112 66355
E-mail: info@newcenturypublications.com

www.newcenturypublications.com

Editorial office:
4800 / 24, Bharat Ram Road,
Ansari Road, Daryaganj,
New Delhi – 110 002

Reprint: 2024

ISBN: **978-81-7708-499-3**

First Published: 2020

Published by New Century Publications and printed at Milan Enterprises, New Delhi.

Designs: Patch Creative Unit, New Delhi.

PRINTED IN INDIA

About the Book

India's 'Act East Policy' has been a significant reorientation in foreign policy towards realizing India's big power ambitions. During the initial years, the focus of the policy was on economic and diplomatic connectivity that cantered around the ASEAN. Since then, the policy has evolved to assume greater strategic dimensions with co-operation in security matters and incremental engagement with countries and regions beyond the ASEAN that include East Asia and the whole of Asia-Pacific.

India's plans to become a global power depend to a great extent on its becoming a dominant economic actor, political and strategic player and soft power attraction in East Asia and Asia-Pacific. This region is the most vibrant economic arena and crucial strategic site in international politics presently.

The changing geopolitical and strategic realities increasingly necessitate a new regional security architecture in the region. Along with its efforts towards economic integration and diplomatic connectivity, India needs to carve out a role in shaping the security structure of the region to deal with issues of maritime disputes and security.

This book is a collection of 7 scholarly papers that discuss various aspects and dimensions of India's Act East Policy.

Editor's Profile

Dr. Josukutty C.A. is currently Associate Professor and Honorary Director, Survey Research Centre, Department of Political Science, University of Kerala. He received his M.A. (Political Science), M.Phil. and Ph.D. degrees from the University of Kerala, India. He was a fellow of the Salzburg Global Seminar, 2007. He was selected to study U.S. foreign policy at the University of Florida in 2010.

Dr. Josukutty was awarded the Fulbright Nehru Academic and Professional Excellence Fellowship in 2015. He has to his credit four books and more than sixty research and popular articles. He has been serving as General Secretary, Association of Political Scientists, Kerala since 2011. His areas of interest and research include international relations, India's foreign policy, Indo-U.S. relations, electoral politics, and human rights.

Contents

Contributors

Srikanth Kondapalli	Centre for East Asian Studies, School of International Studies, Jawaharlal Nehru University (JNU), New Delhi.
P.A. Mathew	Chairman, Grace International Academy, Punalur, Kollam, Kerala.
Muraleedharan Nair	Senior Fellow, Centre for Public Policy Research, Kochi, Kerala.
R.S. Vasan	Director, Chennai Centre for China Studies, Chennai.
Aswani R.S.	Assistant Professor, Department of Public Policy and Administration, University of Petroleum and Energy Studies, Dehradun, Uttarakhand.
Mihir Das	Assistant Professor, Department of Public Policy and Administration, University of Petroleum and Energy Studies, Dehradun, Uttarakhand.
Sally Burt	School of Humanities and Social Sciences, University of New South Wales, Canberra.
Anil Kumar P.	Assistant Professor and Head, Department of Political Science, Panampilly Memorial Government College, Chalakudy, Kerala.

Introduction by the Editor

India's 'Act East Policy' has been a significant reorientation in foreign policy towards realizing India's big power ambitions. During the initial years, the focus of the policy was on economic and diplomatic connectivity that cantered around the ASEAN. Since then, the policy has evolved to assume greater strategic dimensions with cooperation in security matters and incremental engagement with countries and regions beyond the ASEAN that include East Asia and the whole of Asia-Pacific. In 2014, the Government of India made it more active and holistic by integrating it with maritime and strategic objectives. Act East Policy is now envisaged as India's strategic platform for a global role.

India's plans to become a global power depend to a great extent on it becoming a dominant economic actor, political and strategic player and soft power attraction in East Asia and Asia-Pacific. This region is the most vibrant economic arena and crucial strategic site in international politics presently.

The changing geopolitical and strategic realities increasingly necessitate new security architecture in the region. Along with its efforts towards economic integration and diplomatic connectivity, India needs to carve out a role in shaping the security structure of the region to deal with issues of maritime disputes and security. In the recent past, India has established strategic partnerships with all the member countries of ASEAN, and is a party to mechanisms like the ASEAN Defence Minister's Meet, the East Asia Summit and many other regional forums. Simultaneously, India has been progressively cultivating its relationship with small, middle and big powers beyond the ASEAN with the strategic objective of gaining greater clout in the region.

This book is a collection of 7 scholarly papers that discuss various aspects and dimensions of India's Act East Policy.

India's Act East Policy by Srikanth Kondapalli outlines the reasons for initiating the Act East Policy, the dynamics of implementation of such a policy and makes a few broad conclusions to suggest that as a new initiative, this policy coincided with the new government in India since 2014 that is attempting to restructure the inherited structures of foreign and security policies and expand more concretely its scope beyond the Cold War confines of the South Asian region. He examines the economic, connectivity, political, diplomatic, security and cultural dimensions of the Act East Policy and how it is important for India's extended neighbourhood policies in Southeast Asia.

Changing Contours of India's Act East Policy and its Economic Imperatives by P.A. Mathew is an attempt to look at the economic dimensions of India's Act East Policy. It looks at the genesis and implications of the various policies undertaken since the time of India's opening up to the outside world and sees objectively the success of the investment and trade linkages through some specific examples. The paper maps out the linkages in terms of creating an enabling environment for rapid economic development through identification and implementation of specific cooperation projects in trade and investment, industry, technology, human resource development, tourism, agriculture, energy, infrastructure, technology, transport and communications, energy and fisheries etc. in the context of economic imperatives of the Act East Policy.

Act East Policy and the Relevance of the QUAD by Muraleedharan Nair discusses the impact of the QUAD on the balance of power in the region especially in the context of China versus the Quadrilateral. He argues that though the purpose of the QUAD is to ensure a rule based order in the Indo-Pacific, it is indicative of the emergence of a bipolar world order. India becoming a key pillar of it could erode its long-cherished strategic autonomy in foreign affairs and increase cases of tensions with China especially at the borders. Therefore, to avoid the complete distancing of China he advocates that India should engage China in all possible ventures.

Strategic Significance of Bay of Bengal and Andaman and Nicobar Islands in India's Act East Policy by R.S. Vasan examines how the Bay of Bengal, Andaman and Nicobar Islands are in a way central to India's military and strategic counters to China's thrust in India's neighbourhood. The maritime neighbours and spaces in the Bay of Bengal have been targeted for furthering China's economic, military, political and strategic clout. China through its cheque book diplomacy enhanced by the Belt and Road Initiative is a regular sight in Indian waters. India's geographical advantage with the location of Andaman and Nicobar Islands is a critical neutraliser of growing Chinese influence in the region.

Aswani R.S. and Mihir Das in their paper titled *Indian Ocean Region and India's Act East Policy: Maritime Challenges for India in the 21st Century* maintain that India has always considered Indian Ocean as its backyard. But the Indian Ocean Region has always attracted both regional and extra regional powers. The paper argues that China's rapid rise as a great power with extensive cultural and commercial links with Indian Ocean littorals poses immense political and security threats for India. Effective maritime policies are imperative to India's security in its own backyard and integrate its aspirations into the wider spectrum of development, linking East Asia with South Asia. India ought to vigorously pursue extensive economic and defence cooperation with Southeast Asia to counter China and ensure a strong and stable presence in the Indian Ocean Region.

Australia's Perception of India's Act East Policy and its Impact on the Region by Sally Burt is an exploration of India's Act East policy from an Australian perspective. Australia has great concern for several key issues in the Indo-Pacific region. As the recently released foreign policy White Paper suggests, China's rise and balancing the economic relationship with China and the security alliance with the United States are central to Australia's foreign policy in the region. Australia also has a deep and enduring relationship with India based around the export of tertiary education and the ties created by the large contingent of the Indian Diaspora present in Australia's population.

Australia is seeking to build closer economic ties with India and to cooperate on matters of shared interest such as freedom of navigation in the Indian Ocean, and increasing stability through the region's multilateral organisations. Australia welcomes India's Act East Policy and its increasing involvement in strategic collaboration. India's ability to balance China's rise and offer a partnership with Australia based on shared democratic values presents significant opportunities for Australia. India's Act East Policy, which is likely to create greater stability in the region by balancing China's rise, is good for Australia. It also recognises the reduction in vulnerability that comes from the increased interdependence developed in the region by the trade partnerships and multilateral agreements that exist. As such, the friendship between Australia and India is likely to be strengthened as India Acts East and Australia values that friendship deeply.

Japan in India's Act East Policy: Confluence of Interests and Strategy by Anil Kumar P. discusses how the convergence of economic, strategic and geopolitical interests of Japan and India make them crucial allies in the context of the transformations in Southeast Asia and the Act East Policy. He argues that the changing security environment in Southeast Asia exhibits an "order transition" rather than a "power transition" and that opens avenues for soft balancing by India and Japan against the potential fallouts of China's rise. In this context, Japan leverages India's Act East Policy in economic and geopolitical dimensions.

I place on record my deep appreciation and gratitude to all the scholars who have contributed to this volume. Their worthy research papers will surely add to the existing body of literature on the subject.

Thiruvananthapuram **Josukutty C.A.**

1

India's Act East Policy

Srikanth Kondapalli

Ever since the launch of Act East Policy, India's contacts with the extended neighbourhood in Southeast and East Asia has been energized with political, diplomatic, economic and defence cooperation with the countries of these regions. As India celebrated 25 years of interactions with the Southeast Asian grouping the ASEAN, a number of activities were lined up including an unprecedented invitation to the 10 leaders of the region to grace the 69th Indian Republic Day event in January 2018.

While the early 1990s coincided with India's launch of the Look East Policy of attracting capital, exploring markets and expanding people-to-people contact with the Southeast and East Asian regions, and joining various multilateral institutions such as a dialogue partner with the ASEAN in 1996, ASEAN Regional Forum and then the ASEAN Defence Ministerial Meeting+ and East Asian Summit meetings, apart from appointing an ambassador to the ASEAN and enhancing bilateral interactions, today, India's policy is acquiring newer sinews as it is graduating to Act East Policy since November 2014. According to M.J. Akbar, former Minister of State for External Affairs, the key principles and objectives of Act East Policy are modest in nature and are aimed "to promote economic cooperation, cultural ties and develop strategic relationship with countries in the Asia-Pacific region through continuous engagement at bilateral, regional and multilateral levels thereby providing enhanced connectivity to the States of North-Eastern Region with other countries in our neighbourhood". [1]

This paper outlines the reasons for initiating the Act East Policy, the dynamics of implementation of such a policy despite its very recent origin and makes a few broad conclusions to suggest that as a new initiative, this policy coincided with the new government in India since 2014 that is attempting to restructure the inherited structures of foreign and security policies and expand more concretely, its scope beyond the Cold War confines of the South Asian region.

Triggers for Act East Policy

The change in India's policy from Look East to Act East recently has many triggers and suggests a concerted approach towards this region. Firstly, the economic dimension of the relations has come to be the mainstay between the two and specifically under the recent changes in the landscape. Both India and Southeast Asian region have been witnessing relatively high economic growth rates of about 5 to 6 percent annually given the gradual shift from Japan, South Korea, Taiwan and China due to high wages, productivity and domestic consumption. With economic restructuring in India and Southeast Asia, the markets of the region are set to rebound according to various estimates. Specifically, from Southeast Asian region, Vietnam and Indonesia are poised to grow at a higher GDP growth rate for the medium to long-term period. [2]

India and ASEAN signed a free trade agreement in goods and services for mutual benefit in 2009 and 2015, although the former increasingly is concerned with mounting trade deficits. Yet, after the debilitating Asian Financial Crisis of 1997 and the Global Financial Crisis of 2008, both find each other mutually reinforcing and complimentary and hence have embarked on an intensive economic integration process encompassing comprehensive economic partnership. Bilateral trade with the ASEAN is increasing at the rate of nearly 8 percent to make the regional grouping, the 4th largest trading partner for India, although for the ASEAN, India is the 7th largest trading partner. The volume of trade has grown from US$ 5 billion in 1992 to nearly $80 billion with Indonesia and Singapore forming the largest chunk of trade from the region.

Nevertheless, China's trade with the ASEAN is over US$ 400 billion although China began economic engagement with the ASEAN earlier, cobbling up a free trade area in early 2000s. On the other hand, India's investments in the ASEAN countries are higher compared to China by a few billion dollars. With India launching 'Make in India', 'Digital India', unified taxation and maritime connectivity ports under the Sagarmala project, such integrative mechanisms are expected to further intensify.

The recent emphasis in this field includes connectivity projects such as India-Myanmar-Thailand highway which is expected to be completed by 2019 and Kaladanmulti-modal maritime connectivity project. A line of credit of over US$ 1 billion was also offered by India to facilitate physical and digital connectivity with the region. While the Cold War period restricted trade, today North-East India is poised to open up both continental and maritime connections with the ASEAN region benefiting hundreds of millions of marginalized peoples. However, pressing issues such as widespread insurgency, drug trafficking, small arms smuggling and ethnic strife also needs to be addressed by the concerned countries in the region. Yet, North-Eastern portion of India was designated as the primary area of contact in India's Act East Policy. [3]

Secondly, economic relations hinge on the evolving political and diplomatic partnerships. Many of the contentious issues on territorial integrity and sovereignty with Indonesia and Thailand have been resolved by the 1970s, while with Myanmar these issues have never been acute. Thus, compared with others, lack of such contentious issues is a major positive feature in diplomatic interactions. While the ASEAN had certain concerns about the Indian nuclear tests in 1998, long, persuasive and reassuring interactions with the ASEAN partners today has paid off in evolving close relations with the region. In the backdrop of the South China Sea islands dispute that divided and destabilized the ASEAN unity, India's no-historical claims or sovereignty encroachments came as a major reassurance for the ASEAN.

Also, in the backdrop of an assertive China which intends to occupy—in the words of the 19th Communist Party Congress—"Centre Stage" in the global and regional orders at a time of gradual withdrawal of the United States under the Trump Administration, India and ASEAN are apprehensive of negative regional dynamics and hence intend to enhance their relations by coming together. Apart from strengthening bilateral relations, India had upgraded its links to the region in multilateral and sub-regional groupings such as BIMSTEC, [4] Mekong-Ganga Cooperation [5] and others for mutual benefit. India's intent to evolve a mutually beneficial and inclusive security architecture in the region has gone down well with the ASEAN.

Thirdly, India's security assurances to the ASEAN countries and its crucial sea lanes had endeared it to the regional actors. India's position on maritime, cyber and space commons are attracting global attention and commendation. India's stand to abide by The Hague Tribunal ruling awarding disputed islands to Bangladesh has been depicted in sharp contrast to countries grabbing disputed islands by citing unreasonable historical claims. Also, increasingly India has been placing its hard power—the military—at the disposal of natural disaster relief mechanisms. India's prompt assistance during the 2004-05 Tsunami relief operations in Thailand, Indonesia, Myanmar and Sri Lanka, Operation Nargis in Myanmar, offer to address the ever-increasing piracy menace in Southeast Asia as well as port calls, bilateral and multilateral military exercises, offering facilities for training of personnel have all gone well in reassuring the region of India's transparent and benign intentions. India's offer for space tracking stations in Vietnam and Indonesia for data processing on maritime resources, weather forecasting etc., space launch services for Singapore and Malaysia have opened up a new chapter in India-ASEAN relations.

In the backdrop of the contentious dispute over nearly 3 million square km. of maritime territory in the South China Sea, India's suggestions for above board rule-based order, freedom of navigation for uninterrupted flow of commerce, maritime connectivity and common security have all provided much useful backup and alternative for the ASEAN countries. India had also been scaling up its facilities in the Andaman Nicobar Joint Command for possible disaster relief operations in future. The November 11, 2017, revival of Quadrilateral between United States-Japan-India-Australia has suggested the much-needed security assurance to the region, although significant differences exist among the Quad. Also, the Quad needs to intensely work among the ASEAN members and provide reassurances. 15 years of the Declaration of Conduct in the South China Sea has not stopped the 45 disputed islands been encroached. A new Code of Conduct is in the making although this may not be any different from the previous ones as many promises not to militarise the artificial islands have not been observed so far.

On the other hand, concerted militarization of these islands with missile batteries, expansion of air fields, deployment of advanced weapon systems has only led to doubts about any free flow of goods and services through the region. For many countries, this issue has become a grave challenge to their legitimate trade passing through the South China Sea. Regional dominance efforts* in the economic, political and security domains have only alienated it from several ASEAN members. For these reasons of keeping free the sea lanes of communications, piracy and other natural disasters, India-ASEAN interactions on the maritime issues are likely to be placed at a higher pedestal after the economic issues in the short to medium-term.

Fourthly, in increasing India-ASEAN cooperation, the efforts in the cultural field are significant as well. As countries with intensive civilizational interactions, continuous flow of people across the regions for centuries, widespread influence of common religious belief systems with a spill over effect in rich sculptural artefacts, unique dance forms and literature, today, both sides are reviving such links with grand programmes.

Fifthly, the strategic dimension of the Act East Policy is that it coincided with the larger developments in the region which is rechristened as Indo-Pacific, instead of the earlier Asia-Pacific. India's rise in the recent years, its robust democratic process and rule of law, geographical position in the Indian Ocean, rising middle class, sustainable economic growth rates with high domestic consumption, its integration process in the world, IT, software and others, has attracted global attention, specifically of the US and its allies. [6] The January 2015 Obama-Modi joint vision statement on the Indian Ocean and the South China Sea [7] caught global attention although the Indian naval doctrine is based on Indian Ocean as a primary area of responsibility and South China Sea and the Persian Gulf as "secondary".

Nevertheless, China's forays in the South China Sea alerted the Indian side which learnt through the INS Airavat incident in 2009 that freedom of navigation through the region is crucial for the protection of its more than half of global trade passing through these waters. India's alignment with the renewed Quad members is thus visible since November 2017. [8]

Sinews of Act East Policy

The new government in New Delhi since 2014 has been attempting to introduce certain new policies. One of these includes the upgradation of the 1991 Look East Policy into Act East Policy, the latter being formally announced by Prime Minister Narendra Modi in his speech at Naypyidaw in November 2014. [9] Although Act East Policy was mentioned by various others before, after the implementation of the Look East Policy for over two decades, a mid-course correction towards an action-oriented outlook, regional demands and aspirations and change in the context have all necessitated new initiatives by India. [10]

With relatively robust economic growth rates, and prospects for sustaining such growth rates, the new leadership had announced a change in policy from being reactive to one of aspiring to be the "leading power" in global affairs as India's foreign secretary S. Jaishankar suggested in a speech at Singapore in 2015. [11] This necessitates a shift in focus and policy and to provide public goods and services to the neighbourhood and beyond. To cushion such a policy is to invoke the diplomatic, commercial and military resources of the country in a coordinated manner. Many of the visits undertaken by PM Modi in the first two years of assuming office since mid-2014 were towards the East and include visits to Japan in September 2014 and November 2016, Myanmar, Singapore, Fiji, South Korea, Mongolia, Vietnam, Australia and others.

The key issues in the Act East Policy, according to Minister of State Gen. V.K. Singh, in a reply to a query in the lower house of the Indian Parliament, (much like his colleague cited above) is "to promote economic cooperation, cultural ties and develop strategic relationship with countries in the Asia-Pacific region through continuous engagement at bilateral, regional and multilateral levels thereby providing enhanced connectivity to the States of North-Eastern Region with other countries in our neighbourhood". [12]

According to the Ministry of Defence, in its annual report of 2016, ...under the 'Act East' policy which places renewed emphasis on engagement with Asia-Pacific, India has been an active participant in various bilateral as well as multilateral fora with a focus on security matters such as the East Asia Summit, ADMM Plus and ASEAN Regional Forum (ARF). There is also a need to further improve regional responses to challenges such as transnational crime, terrorism, natural disasters, pandemics, cyber security as well as food and energy security. [13]

Speaking at the gathering of over 30 countries at Singapore meeting on the Indian Ocean on September 1, 2016, former Minister of State for External Affairs M.J. Akbar suggested that India occupies a unique position between the Phoenix Horizon towards its east with high growth rates and the Toxin Horizon of conflict, war and terrorism towards its west. The strategic choice for India then is clear of veering towards the east. [14]

Geographically, while India borders Myanmar in the continental domain and in the maritime domain with Thailand and Indonesia, Act East Policy is acquiring more sinews with distant Japan with which India for a long time had summit level meetings between the leaderships.

Recently, India and Japan further elevated these ties towards a 21st century partnership. Apart from the 2+2 dialogue mechanism (between foreign and defence ministries), which strengthened mutual understanding on a number of issues, both have been intensifying relations in the field of defence, bilateral economic and technological fields reinforced by comprehensive economic partnership, and other fields. PM Modi made his first visit to Tokyo in September 2014 outside the South Asian region. Japan is also one of the largest investors in India with over 1300 companies basing their operations in India. Further, Japan is upgrading Indian infrastructure projects by connecting Mumbai with Delhi through a dedicated freight corridor and is committed to build a high-speed railway from Ahmedabad to Mumbai. Both are also exploring defence cooperation, with maritime region between the two becoming the focus. Japan as well has joined the trilateral Malabar naval exercises between the US and India since December 2015. Japan's "free and open Indo-Pacific" policy is being aligned with India's Act East Policy, with specific infrastructure project being undertaken by Japan in North-East India. [15]

Another country that has become crucial is South Korea which also plays a significant role in the Act East Policy of India. Since 2009, relations were upgraded to include maritime cooperation, defence technology transfers and commercial cooperation in the comprehensive economic partnership arrangement. Soon after China's denial of a visa to an Indian Army General hailing from Jammu and Kashmir region in mid-2009, India considered it fit to elevate ties with Seoul in September that year. PM Modi visited Seoul in June 2015 and South Korean President visited India in quick succession.

The key to the success of both the Look East and Act East policies, however, is the "land bridge" connectivity between India and the Southeast Asian region through Myanmar. Although this link is straddled with a number of problems such as relations with the military junta till recently, insurgency in the North-East region and others, India had approached this aspect through a multipronged approach. Today, India had evolved strategic partnerships with a number of countries in Asia-Pacific region, including ASEAN, Australia, Japan, Indonesia, Vietnam, Malaysia, South Korea and Singapore.

At the multilateral level, besides intensifying relations with ASEAN Regional Forum and East Asian Summit, India had undertaken new initiatives such as Bay of Bengal Initiative for Multi-sectoral Technical and Economic Cooperation (BIMSTEC), Asia Cooperation Dialogue, Mekong-Ganga Cooperation and Indian Ocean Rim Association ASEAN Defence Ministers' Meeting and others.

In the recent times, the number of visits of high level leadership has increased. Former PM Manmohan Singh visited Myanmar in 2012, followed by other visits by the military and the local leaders from North-East. PM Modi visited Naypyidaw in November 2014, reciprocated by State Councillor Aug San Suu Kyi in late 2016. [16]

While both India and China joined the ASEAN process since the 1990s, and both agreed to ASEAN being the "driver" in all the processes and agreed to the ASEAN conditions of Treaty of Amity and nuclear weapon free zone for the region, China of late has been asserting its position partly due to the sovereignty claims over the contiguous South China Sea as well as in the leadership contest with the US and Japan over the region. As India has no sovereignty claims in the region, and despite ASEAN's initial negative responses towards Indian nuclear tests in 1998, many in the ASEAN see India as a balancer and provider of security to the region. After the July 12, 2016 Hague Tribunal ruling, China had also changed its position on ASEAN by increasingly following a divide and rule policy in the grouping. [17]

Connectivity

For further economic integration and providing substance to the Act East Policy, India had of late been emphasizing on the connectivity with the ASEAN region through road, railways and maritime port links through the North-East region. [18] The main projects include Kaladan Multi-modal Transit Transport Project, the India-Myanmar-Thailand Trilateral Highway Project, Rhi-Tiddim Road Project, and Border Haats. The June 17, 2016 joint statement between India and Thailand noted the progress made in the India-Myanmar-Thailand Trilateral Highway connecting Moreh in Manipur to Mae Sot in Thailand through Myanmar. [19]

According to Asian Development Bank on the multi-infrastructure projects coming up in the Asia-Pacific region, the benefits are numerous. It mentions about the 90 km. Imphal-Moreh road constructed at a cost of US$ 160 million, in addition to a railway project of over 95 km. at a cost of US$ 400 million. In addition, there is also the Chennai port elevated expressway and Sagar Island Deepwater port at Kolkata (estimated to cost US$ 1.3 billion). In Bangladesh, the new Sonadiya Deepwater Port is expected to cost over US$ 1 billion. Myanmar has also embarked on several projects, including the Tamu-Kalay (127 km. rail project costing US$ 98 million), and Kalay-Mandalay (539 km. rail project costing US$ 162 million). In addition, the Myanmar to Thailand road projects involving the different lines of Endu-Kawkareik-Myawaddy-Yagyi-Kalewa-Tamu-Mae Sot project connects India's North-East to Thailand. [20]

Military Dimensions

The "action" oriented aspect of Act East Policy includes the deployment of the armed forces in the Asia-Pacific region. This has been a significant change in the Indian postures given its traditional policy of independent foreign policy, non-alignment, no military troops or bases abroad. Today, India is actively engaging with the outside world both in the West and the East, with specific emphasis on Act East Policy. PM Modi had initiated several programmes including "Sagarmala" to enhance the maritime infrastructure projects across the Indian coasts, and "Project Mausam" for connecting the Indian Ocean littorals for commercial and cultural contacts. These are also part of the overall 'Make in India', 'Digital India' initiatives undertaken by the government since 2014.

At one time, India was a part of the counter-terrorism support operations at Ainee in Tajikistan. In addition to Haiphong and Nha Trang in Vietnam where Indian naval ships could dock, they also have access to Subic Bay and Clark Air Base in the Philippines. With PM Modi's "Indian Ocean Diplomacy" initiative in 2014, Indian ships have been planning replenishment facilities at Agaléga Islands in Mauritius, and in northern Mozambique. Recently, as well with the construction of the Chabahar port in Iran, India intends to connect to the energy-rich Central Asian Republics. In 2007, the Indian armed forces have adopted the posture of Indian Ocean as their primary focus while South China Sea and beyond being of secondary importance. In 2015, this posture was acknowledged as the national policy. Act East

Policy is thus subservient to this overall national policy of considering Indian Ocean as being of utmost importance for the country. India intends to usher in its "leading" role in the region.

Vietnam is considered to be a "central pillar" in India's Act East Policy, specifically in defence ties. [21] Both countries have embarked upon comprehensive mutual support with Vietnam providing urban counter-terrorism training to the Indian forces, while India assisting Vietnam in training in Kilo-class submarine operations, SU-30 aircraft and other platforms, in addition to toying with the idea of supplying to Vietnam, the Brahmos cruise missiles and fast attack crafts. Also, Vietnam has granted the Indian naval forces, permanent berthing facilities for visiting ships at Haiphong and Nha Trang in Vietnam. During PM Modi's visit to Hanoi in late 2016, it was agreed that India will provide Vietnam with a greater credit line, expanded from the September 2014 figure of US$ 100 million, to over US$ 500 million. In addition, India had been preparing to manufacture defence items in Vietnam for export. Vietnam has also agreed to provide facilities for satellite link-up facilities for India. In addition to the energy sector cooperation where both the state-owned ONGC Videsh Limited and private sector Essar have started drilling operations in South China Sea, bilateral cooperation fields are expanding substantially between India and Vietnam.

Indian armed forces conduct a variety of military engagements with a number of counterparts in the Asia-Pacific region. These include the participation in Langkawi International Maritime Aerospace Exhibition (LIMA), an annual event in Malaysia; International Maritime Defence Expo (IMDEX) Asia at Singapore, ASEAN Regional Forum Disaster Relief Exercises in Malaysia, and International Fleet Review at Sagami Bay, Japan. As a part of the Eastern Fleet Overseas Deployment, Indian naval ships were deployed in South China Sea in May-June 2015 and participated in the SIMBEX events with Singapore, and PASSEX with their counterparts in Indonesia, Australia, Thailand and Cambodia. Indian Navy also conducts coordinated patrols (CORPAT) with its counterparts in Myanmar, Thailand and Indonesia, in addition to being an "Observer Plus" in the Cobra Gold multilateral exercises. [22]

With Australia, Indian navy has been conducting AUSINDEX exercises since 2015 for enhancing maritime security, cooperation and interoperability. Indian armed forces have also been involved in pitching their hard power in the natural disaster relief measures in the Asia-Pacific region. These include dispatching 27 ships and 5,000 personnel for providing relief and evacuation of victims during the Tsunami of 2004-05 in Indonesia, Thailand, Sri Lanka, Maldives and other regions, involvement in "Operation Nargis" in Myanmar for relief measures, and the like. The agreement with Indonesia in May 2018 for developing Sabang port is a major development in the Act East Policy. [23]

The annual Malabar Exercises almost being uninterruptedly conducted with the United States naval forces since the early 1990s, has become a trilateral event since 2015 with the participation of the Japanese Self Defence Maritime Forces. In September 2007, all the three, in addition to Australia and Singapore joined the exercise in the Bay of Bengal but were discontinued with China's demarches. It appears that such multilateral naval exercises could commence in the near future.

On November 23, 2015, speaking at the Shangri La, PM Modi observed that one of the main drivers of the recently enacted Act East Policy include efforts to enforce freedom of navigation in the high seas. This observation comes in the wake of "territorial sea" proponents in the South China Sea that intends to create enclaves and possible restrictions on free trade passages in the region. [24]

However, while the Obama-Modi joint vision statement of January 2015 called for consolidation of positions in the Indian Ocean and the South China Sea, the latter region is more complicated given the Chinese assertiveness in the region despite the July 12, 2016 judgement by the Permanent Court of Arbitration at The Hague quashing several sovereignty claims in the region. The United States want India to play a "lynchpin" role and as a "net security provider" in the Indo-Pacific region. While the above details suggest that the Indian armed forces have been active in the Act East Policy, sensitivities were expressed on "joint patrolling" in the South China Sea region. This has been part of an ongoing dialogue among several stakeholders in the region.

In his speech at the Shangri La meeting in Singapore on June 1, 2018, PM Modi had stressed almost all the six aspects of the main themes under discussion at the November 11, 2017 Quadrilateral Security Dialogue among officials of India, US, Japan and Australia, viz., open and free international system, rule of law, freedom of navigation and over flight, maritime security and connectivity and counter-terrorism. In addition, he suggested to an "inclusive" architecture with ASEAN centrality. [25]

Observations

Thus, India's Act East Policy has reinvigorated its ties to the Indo-Pacific region. Diplomatic, political, commercial, defence, people-to-people and cultural contacts have increased between India and its eastern neighbours stretching from Japan and Fiji to Maldives. The number of high-level political visits increased recently bringing in its wake an increasing understanding on a number of issues of mutual concern. Given the lack of any territorial ambitions on the part of India and showcasing its economic potential in the recent times with high growth rates had all attracted India to the East and Southeast Asian countries. Making available its hard power for disaster relief and other humanitarian measures has further solidified relations with these two regions. However, the unfolding of Act East Policy has its own dissonances, mainly from China whose rise in the last three decades is altering the regional order.

Thus, there is a potential for competition or even conflict in overlapping areas—such as South China Sea—between these two Asian giants, in addition to the role of Japan which is also retrieving its lost ground in the recent times. While India-China conflict is muted currently, competition for influence in the region is visible, although both have mutually beneficial economic relations in addition to conflict preventive confidence building measures.

On the other hand, India and Japan (and Singapore) have been intensifying cooperation on a range of issues, including on how to counter an aggressive Chinese posture. They support a rules-based order, including freedom of navigation in the maritime regions. Primarily intended to protect the burgeoning economic and trade links with the east, India's Act East Policy is also acquiring teeth with the increasing engagement of the Indian armed forces with many of their counterparts in the region.

When the Quad was formed in November 2017, Indian foreign ministry stated that they [the Quad officials] agreed that a free, open, prosperous and inclusive Indo-Pacific region serves the long-term interests of all countries in the region and of the world at large. The officials also exchanged views on addressing common challenges of terrorism and proliferation linkages impacting the region as well as on enhancing connectivity. [26]

The above suggests that while India has expressed its interest in the Indo-Pacific idea and had committed several resources, such efforts are expressed through its own policies such as the Act East Policy, although the trilateral Malabar exercises can be termed as a concrete expression of this initiative. Thus, while the erstwhile Look East Policy provided for economic and commercial linkages between India and Southeast and East Asian countries, the recent Act East Policy since 2014 is focused on diplomatic, economic, security and cultural relations thus providing for a comprehensive package for Indian interactions with the region.

Notes and References

1. M.J. Akbar replying to a parliament question. See "Question Number 26, Act East Policy" February 2, 2017, available at: http://www.mea.gov.in/rajyasabha.htm?dtl/27982/question+no26+act+east+policy.
2. "Shift of global economic power to emerging economies set to continue in long run, with India, Indonesia and Vietnam among star performers", PricewaterhouseCoopers, February 7, 2017, available at:
https://www.pwc.com/jp/en/press-room/world-in-2050-3.html.
3. In October 2015, when the External Affairs Ministry convened the Governors of the North Eastern states at New Delhi, Minister Sushma Swaraj stated that the region is "natural partner in India's Act East Policy", being our land bridge to ASEAN, and the Act East Policy is a means to strengthen the stability, economy and prospects of our North-Eastern region". See "Briefing session hosted by External Affairs Minister for the Governors of North-Eastern States on India's Act East Policy", October 6, 2015, available at: http://www.mea.gov.in/press-releases.htm?dtl/25897/briefing+session+hosted+by+external+affairs+minister+for+the+governors+of+north+eastern+states+on+indias+act+east+policy+october+06+2015. Later, in 2018, the Minister, in a session with the Chief Ministers meeting from the region, stated that the state governments from this region are "stakeholders" for the Act East Policy. See "Press Release on EAM's Interactive Session with the Chief Ministers of the North Eastern States on Act East Policy" May 4, 2018, available at: http://www.mea.gov.in/press-releases.htm?dtl/29865/press+release+on+eams+interactive+session+with+the+chief+ministers+of+the+north+eastern+states+on+act+east+policy.
4. The Bay of Bengal Initiative for Multi-Sectoral Technical and Economic Cooperation (BIMSTEC) was founded in 1997 by seven nations (Nepal, Bhutan, Bangladesh, India, Sri Lanka, Myanmar and Thailand) and is home to 1.5 billion people and a GDP of nearly US$ 3 trillion. Its focus is on connectivity, transportation, tourism, agriculture, environmental protection, countering terrorism and transnational crime, energy, disaster relief etc. India had upgraded the BIMSTEC partly due to the inability of the SAARC to deliver on various fronts as well as to

connect to high growth rate regions of ASEAN. As a host of the BRICS summit meeting at Goa, India invited the BIMSTEC leaders for the summit in October 2016.

5. Mekong-Ganga Cooperation between six nations (Laos, Cambodia, Vietnam, Thailand, Myanmar and India) was formed in 2000 and promotes, tourism, culture, education and transportation.
6. "US warmly welcomes India's Act East Policy", Business Standard, November 7, 2014, available at: https://www.business-standard.com/article/pti-stories/us-warmly-welcomes-india-s-act-east-policy-114110700289_1.html.
7. The 2015 statement mentioned that "India's 'Act East Policy and the United States' rebalance to Asia provide opportunities for India, the United States, and other Asia-Pacific countries to work closely to strengthen regional ties, the Leaders announced a Joint Strategic Vision to guide their engagement in the region". See "Joint Statement during the visit of President of USA to India" January 25, 2015, available at: http://mea.gov.in/bilateral-documents.htm?dtl/24726/Joint_Statement_during_the_visit_of_President_of_USA_to_India_Shared_Effort_Progress_for_All.
8. See Rajiv Bhatia and Vijay Sakhuja, (2014) (eds.), "Indo-Pacific Region: Political and Strategic Prospects", New Delhi: Vij Books and Brahma Chellaney, "A New Order for the Indo-Pacific" March 9, 2018, available at: <https://www.project-syndicate.org/commentary/china-indo-pacific-security-framework-by-brahma-chellaney-2018-03.
9. "'Look East Policy now turned into Act East Policy: Modi", *The Hindu*, November 13, 2014, available at: http://www.thehindu.com/news/national/look-east-policy-now-turned-into-act-east-policy-modi/article6595186.ece.
10. See Amitandu Palit (2016), "India's Act East Policy and Implications for Southeast Asia", *Southeast Asian Studies*, pp. 81-91 and Danielle Rajendram (2014), "India's New Asia-Pacific Strategy: Modi Acts East", Lowy Institute, December, available at: https://www.lowyinstitute.org/sites/default/files/indias-new-asia-pacific-strategy-modi-acts-east_0.pdf.

11. "Speech by Dr. S. Jaishankar, Foreign Secretary to mark 25 years of India-Singapore Partnership at Shangri La Hotel, Singapore" July 11, 2017, available at: <http://www.mea.gov.in/Speeches-Statements.htm?dtl/28609/speech+by+dr+s+jaishankar+foreign+secretary+to+mark+25+years+of+indiasingapore+partnership+at+shangri+la+hotel+singapore+july+11+2017.
12. See "Look East and Act East Policy", Unstarred Question No. 3121, March 16, 2016, available at: http://mea.gov.in/lok-sabha.htm?dtl/26554/question+no+3121+look+east+and+act+east+policy.
13. Ministry of Defence, Government of India, Annual Report, 2016, New Delhi, p. 4, available at: http://www.mod.nic.in/writereaddata/Annual2016.pdf.
14. See "Welcome Remarks by Minister of State for External Affairs M.J. Akbar at the Inaugural Session of Indian Ocean Conference", September 1, 2016, available at: http://mea.gov.in/SpeecheStatements.htm?dtl/27ber+01+2016.
15. See "Launch of India-Japan Act East Forum", December 5, 2017, available at: http://www.mea.gov.in/press-releases.htm?dtl/29154/launch+of+indiajapan+act+east+forum.
16. For the recent visits of the President to Vietnam in September 2014, PM Modi to Naypyidaw in November 2014 and Foreign Minister Sushma Swaraj to Vietnam, Singapore and Myanmar see Manish Chand, "Act East: India's ASEAN Journey" November 14, 2014, available at: http://mea.gov.in/in-focus-article.htm?24216/Act+East+Indias+ASEAN+Journey.
17. India's position on South China Sea, as articulated in various official statements, include that the sovereignty dispute need to be resolved in a bilateral fashion by the disputants, that to usher in peace and stability in the region crucial for free passage of goods and services, the concerned understandings including the Declaration of the Conduct since 2002 and the relevant multilateral institutions should be given full play, and international law including the 1982 UNCLOS be observed by all parties. After the July 2016 verdict, India suggested to all parties to the dispute that "utmost respect to the UNCLOS"

provisions be observed in South China Sea. Given over 55 percent of Indian trade passing through the region, it is natural that India had supported freedom of navigation principle, specifically after the 2009 INS Airavat incident.

18. See Namrata Goswami (2009), "Looking "East" Through India's North East-Identifying Policy "Challenges" and Outlining the "Responses", IDSA Occasional Paper No. 2, June.
19. "India-Thailand Joint Statement during the visit of Prime Minister of Thailand to India", June 17, 2016, available at: http://mea.gov.in/bilateral-documents.htm?dtl/26923/indiathailand+joint+statement+during+the+visit+of+prime+minister+of+thailand+to+india.
20. This is based on Asian Development Bank report, available at: https://www.adb.org/sites/default/files/publication/174393/regional-transport-infrastructure.pdf. See also the various infrastructure projects coming up in the Asia-Pacific region in the recent times, available at: https://reconnectingasia.csis.org/map.
21. On the eve of PM Modi's visit to Hanoi, just before the Hangzhou G-20 Summit meeting, in September 2016, Indian foreign ministry's Secretary (East) suggested that Vietnam forms the "central pillar". See "Vietnam a 'central pillar' of India's Act East Policy, government says as Narendra Modi begins visit" September 2, 2016, available at: http://scroll.in/latest/815579/vietnam-a-central-pillar-of-indias-act-east-policy-government-says-as-narendra-modi-begins-visit.
22. Ministry of Defence, Government of India, Annual Report 2016, New Delhi, pp. 29-32, available at: http://www.mod.nic.in/writereaddata/Annual2016.pdf.
23. The agreement between Indonesia and India stated that both will explore "convergences and complementarities in the region between India's Act East Policy and Security and Growth for all in the Region (SAGAR), and Indonesian Ocean Policy and Indonesia's Global Maritime Fulcrum Vision". See "Shared Vision of India-Indonesia Maritime Cooperation in the Indo-Pacific" May 30, 2018, available at: http://www.mea.gov.in/bilateral-documents.htm?dtl/29933/shared+vision+of+indiaindonesia+maritime+cooperation+in+the+indopacific.

24. "Modi lays out India's Act East policy in Singapore Lecture at the Shangri La", *The Straits Times*, November 23, 2015, available at: http://www.straitstimes.com/singapore/modi-lays-out-indias-act-east-policy-in-singapore-lecture-at-the-shangri-la.
25. "Prime Minister's Keynote Address at Shangri La Dialogue" June 1, 2018, available at: http://www.mea.gov.in/Speeches-Statements.htm?dtl/29943/prime+ministers+keynote+address+at+shangri+la+dialogue+june+01+2018.
26. "India-Australia-Japan-U.S. Consultations on Indo-Pacific November 12, 2017", available at: http://mea.gov.in/press-releases.htm?dtl/29110/IndiaAustraliaJapanUS_Consultations_on_IndoPacific_November_12_2017.

2

Changing Contours of India's Act East Policy and its Economic Imperatives

P.A. Mathew

Introduction

As the era of economic liberalisation and globalisation makes the world borderless, the range and scope of regional economic cooperation has increased tremendously among countries of different regions. The high level of economic interdependence between economies reflects the historical advancement of the world's economic and political regulation (Carbaugh, 2008). Due to the pressures of globalisation, nations across the world are seeking greater efficiency through larger markets, increased competition, access to superior technology, and greater investment channels through Regional Integration arrangements (RIAs).

Within such arrangements, there is also desire to assist neighbouring nations for mutually beneficial reasons, as well as to take anticipatory action against the spill over of unrest and mass economic migration.

Asia-Pacific as a region of critical global significance, both strategically and economically, is beyond contestation. In the last two decades, Asia-Pacific has transformed from a region to a global actor and it has become the centre of global supply chain. It has also become the crux of the world growth trajectory and home to 3.6 billion people constituting 51 percent of the world's population. This remarkable transformation of the Asian economies and the anticipated tectonic shift in global power similar to the one that took place in the early 20th century, in which the countries of the Indo-

Pacific will begin to dominate global economics, politics and security is often termed as '21st century to be the Asian century' (Madhubani, 2009).

From the East Asian Miracle to Asian Financial Crisis of the 1997-98 to Emergence of China and India as the leading countries in terms of economic development, Asian countries have come a long way. This is all the more important because the transformation happened in the context of globalisation which as a process had spread far and wide starting with the later part of the 20th century to the first decades of the 21st century to almost all corners of the globe.

A combination of economic, strategic, and domestic considerations has led India to pay greater attention to its eastern neighbours since the 1990s. India's steadily growing ties with East and Southeast Asian countries have become an increasingly important element of India's foreign policy. India is working with these countries bilaterally as well as through regional frameworks like the East Asia Summit (EAS), Asia-Europe Meeting (ASEM), and Association of Southeast Nations (ASEAN), and sub-regional organizations like Bay of Bengal Initiative for Multi-Sectoral Technical and Economic Cooperation (BIMSTEC) and Mekong-Ganga Cooperation. The main driver remains economic, and India has many ongoing and planned Free trade Agreements (FTAs) with the countries of this region. Of late, defence and security ties too have grown (Rajiv Sikri, 2009).

Rise of China and Look East Policy

As the world moves into the second decade of the 21st century, the fundamental change characterising the geopolitical reality of the world is the rise of China both in terms of capacity as well as ambitions to shape the global and regional structures of power. The rise can be seen from various angles but the obvious is manifested in China's growing ability to pursue strategic interests not only in the geographically contiguous areas but also in areas as far and wide as Australia,

Africa and Americas. This is all the more pertinent because the advanced western countries have been facing economic shocks at regular intervals. China has witnessed continuous growth in its GDP growth rate, rapidly reducing its distance with the largest economy of the world—The United States of America. China as the second largest consumer of global energy goes on to explore newer supply sources and develop better connectivity with them, creating in the process, a new vision of global outreach. China has become indispensable for any deliberation over the management or restructuring of the system of global order, in existence for the last 100 years.

China's rise as a global player has amplified new changes at the regional and continental level. There are new sets of relationships emerging, marked by parallel trends towards cooperation and confrontation. There are mixed feelings of greater understanding and mistrust between different states but with enormous economic resources and political capital at its disposal, China has been able to manage its affairs with finesse. While the economic component of the rise of China offers optimism for sustained growth stories in Asia, its strategic dimension brings forth an element of uncertainty, especially with regard to an incipient great power rivalry, possible efforts towards domination and redrawing of boundaries.

On the other hand, the spectre of great power politics is gaining momentum in the Asia-Pacific. The two forces, one represented by China in terms of its strategic ambition and influence and the other represented by two powerful neighbours Japan and India and their continued balancing act pose a massive challenge to maintaining peace and stability in Southeast Asia. It is this mixed baggage of excitement and anxiety which is the background to the much talked about Look East-Act East Policy of India and its economic imperatives. India' Look East Policy of the 1991 to Act East Policy of the recent times has to be understood in the context of changes in Asia especially with regard to the East Asian Miracle, Asian economic crisis of 1997 and the rise of China.

As the Indian economy transforms from a local and regional player to a transnational player, the Look East-Act East Policy raises important historical and geopolitical questions. There will be questions with regard to India's credibility to assume the role of a leader in Asia. Although China has emerged as the largest trading partner for a majority of the countries in Southeast Asia and there has been an increasing people-to-people interaction, economic cooperation and high level of inter-governmental relationships, through the Look East/Act East policy, India is making an attempt to spread its own influence in the region.

Southeast Asia and India: Civilizational Heritage and Historical Trading Links

The civilisation of India influenced languages, scripts, written tradition, literature, calendars, belief systems and artistic aspects of Southeast Asia. The spread of Indian cultural influences led to the cultural enrichment of Southeast Asian countries and undoubtedly constitutes a glorious chapter in Southeast Asian and Indian history alike. Indianised Kingdoms like Funan, Sri Kshetra, Pagan, Khemer, Sri Vijaya, Sailentra and Majapahit, the familiar Indo-Sanskrit vocabulary in Thai language and Bahasa Indonesia; architectural monuments like Angkar, Pagan, Borobudur and Lara Djon ggrong; literary masterpieces like Ramakein, Amaramala, Arjuna Vivaha and Bharata Yudha, the Wajang Kulit are based on the Ramayana and Mahabharata traditions.

During the early centuries of Christian era, Roman trade dominated the Indian Ocean. Both Southeast Asia and India were part of the world trading network and trade relations between both of them flourished during this period. Seafaring traders and missionaries from India carried Hindu-Buddhist ideas to the elites of Southeast Asia over a period of time. There were spread of ideas and concepts and in particular were the acceptance of Kingship and notions of divinity by Southeast Asia (Frost, 2009). By 500 A.D., Sanskrit had been accepted widely in Southeast Asia and was frequently the official language of the court.

Much of the interaction between Indian and maritime Southeast Asian economies were driven by interest in the trade of the South China Sea and Eastern Seas of Indonesia. Thus, the Southeast Asian trade was entirely dependent upon Indian Ocean and South China Sea. In the first three centuries of the Christian era, the trading relations with India was established by the distribution of Roman-Indian Rouletted pottery at a few coasts including North coasts of Java, Bali and the coast of central Vietnam. The Southeast Asian trade is well documented after seventh century onwards. The seventh and eighth centuries AD witnessed expansion in the volume of Asian sea trade involving maritime Southeast, due to Chinese interest and parallel rise in the demand from the prosperous centres on the East Coast of India.

British rule in India and division of Southeast Asian countries in the hands of different colonial powers like Dutch, French, and Portuguese, suspended continuous interaction which was in existence for more than 2,000 years between the region and India. As a result of this change in power, commercial interaction which was in existence for a long period of time between the two regions was subordinated to the political and strategic consideration of the colonial powers.

This breakdown of commercial interaction was important because what it changed was the traditional modes of commodities which were exchanged over a long time which influenced the pattern of living in both the regions. It also led to impoverishment for people who were dependant on this trade for centuries through successive generations. Through the years of colonial rule, these powers benefited hugely from the large market for their finished goods and as a source of raw material for the industrial production. This was the case of both India and Southeast Asian region. It also led to the breakdown of traditional modes of production and the decimation of the local industries. The industrial backwardness of both the regions during the colonial period was same although it was ruled by different colonial powers.

Although prior to independence of India, occasion to meet leaders from Southeast Asia was limited, for few nationalist leaders especially Jawaharlal Nehru, the Brussels Congress of the Oppressed Nationalities in 1927 provided an occasion for meeting with the leaders fighting the French and Dutch colonial exploitation in Southeast Asia. There was a tacit understanding that problems of both the regions were the same due to the colonial rule (Misra, 1994).

Indian Independence and After

India's independence was one of the greatest landmarks of contemporary world history. The relevance of that event was not only about a country of large population gaining the right to decide its own destiny; it was also about a pattern being created across the world creating unique and far-reaching changes in the world power structure. It led to the breakup of colonial system and resulted in the emergence of Afro-Asian nations to the forefront.

India's policy towards Southeast Asia in the early years of independence, more precisely until the late 50s was dynamic, forward looking and was in complete empathy and solidarity with the hopes and aspirations of the Southeast Asian people (Surya Narayanan, 1996). Even with colonial rule breaking down the traditional commercial connection between the two regions, it is interesting to note India depended on Southeast Asia for many products which were important. In 1950-51, India imported 50 percent of its rice, 17 percent of its petroleum, 8 percent of its metals and 4 percent of its timber requirements from Southeast Asia. However, there have been curious fluctuations in Indian trade figures with Southeast Asia. In 1951-52, it dropped down to 7 percent.

It is interesting to look into the reasons for the shift in trade between both the regions during this period. This is a relevant question to be raised in the context of India again trying to build bridges with Southeast Asia in the 1990s through Look East and later through Act East Policy.

There are many arguments to justify this change. During the late fifties and early sixties, India's framework of development that combined both democracy and mixed economy was seen as a model of economic development by many Southeast Asian countries. This admiration evaporated in the late sixties and early seventies as India faltered on the economic front. Trade was a reflection of change in perception of Southeast countries towards India.

One of the arguments regarding the shift is the fact that many parts of Southeast Asia were plagued by political turmoil and instability. Some of the states were still under the control of the colonial powers and their directives could be the reason for a fall in trade. It is also argued that until 1957 only Burma, the Philippines, Indonesia, Thailand and Cambodia were independent. Insurgencies were a problem in Burma, Philippines and Indonesia and Vietnam was only nominally independent.

There are strong reasons to understand the fall in trade to the indifference and lack of interest on the part of Government of India. The political class and the civil servants in power in Delhi immediately after the Independence had their education in western countries and looked up to the west as a model for India's growth. This resulted in forging closer economic ties with western capitalist countries at the cost of trade with Southeast Asia.

The period after this has been a period of downhill for India's economic relations with Southeast Asia although there were several plus points. Historically, Burma, Thailand, Malaysia, Indonesia, Laos and Cambodia have been deeply influenced by Indian political ideas, religion, art and language. Although India during the period of struggle for independence and since her Independence, visualized an 'Asian Union based on 'Asianism' comprising of countries of Asia, the first Asian Relations Conference in 1947 was not very encouraging to promote the idea. Bandung Conference of 1955 was a watershed in India's relations with Southeast Asia as a whole. From then, it is generally regarded that a sort of stagnation developed in her relations with countries of the region and her global involvement became more evident in her foreign policy.

It was also believed that Government of India tended to take the friendship and goodwill of the Southeast Asians for granted and did not take any concrete steps to keep it alive and progressing. It is also felt that India did not bother to do anything to arrest the trends which were going against the interests of the country in some of the Southeast Asian countries during the period. Indian contribution to the debate on the important political and strategic subjects in the region like declaration of Indian Ocean as a zone of peace, freedom of navigation in the Malacca Straits, neutralization of Southeast Asia and the formation of ASEAN were developments of significance. But Indians remained on the periphery and their contributions were negligible. This attitude of remaining passive spectators rather than interested participants during the crucial period in the economic history of Southeast Asia in the hindsight has been a diplomatic blunder because Southeast Asia was beginning to take off economically and if India had joined the bandwagon then, the economic life of people of India would have been different.

The main feature of Indira Gandhi's policy towards the ASEAN was that in the face of hurdles in Indo-China relations, it was better to improve bilateral relations with individual ASEAN countries. During the period 1966-68, India signed direct bilateral agreements for technical and economic co-operation with Southeast Asian countries (Indonesia, Malaysia, the Philippines and Thailand) rather than through the ASEAN.

During her visit to Malaysia, Indira Gandhi, the then Prime Minister of India, firmly reiterated India's support to regional cooperation in Asia. She also suggested that regional cooperation in Southeast Asia would be made viable only on broader regional basis. The main purpose of Indira Gandhi's visit was to discuss the increased economic and technical co-operation among the countries of Southeast Asia. India tried for membership of the ASEAN, but the proposition remained totally unacceptable as the ASEAN Declaration did not provide for any country from outside the Southeast Asia region to be eligible for membership. It is also believed that at that time the ASEAN countries had a fear of being dominated by a big country like India if they made India a member of that organization.

An attempt made by India to engage closely with Southeast Asia economically during this period was the proposal for an economic grouping called the Economic and Social Commission for Asia and Far East (ECAFE). The founding members of the Association of Southeast Asian Nations (ASEAN)—Malaysia, Singapore, Indonesia, the Philippines and Thailand—however did not pay much attention to this grouping because of the divergent stand of India and South Asian countries on various issues.

If there is one incident which could be considered as a crucial factor which made the economic relationship between India and Southeast Asia to go down further, it is the India-Soviet Treaty of Peace, Friendship and Co-operation signed in New Delhi on August, 9, 1971. Although conclusion of Indo-Soviet Treaty was considered as a remarkable achievement for Indian foreign policy, reactions outside India raised a number of questions about its nature and implications. Has India abandoned the policy of non-alignment and if it was a defence pact or a mutual defence treaty were serious questions which had no definite answers. Both India and Southeast Asia followed divergent paths more visibly since then.

They found themselves advocating different economic strategies and supporting distinct political ideologies and this became crystal clear when India supported Vietnam's invasion of Cambodia in 1979, while ASEAN condemned it as a blatant violation of the organization's sacred non-intervention principle (Acharya, 2009). India missed historic opportunities to engage in fruitful dialogue with Southeast Asian countries in 1975 and 1980, refusing them twice and labelling them as allies of the imperialist west (Anand, 2009).

East Asian Miracle and its Ramifications

One of the most important developments which made India look up to Asia again was the impressive growth of many economies in East Asia since the 1960s. There is no doubt that since 1960, East Asia has become richer faster than any other region of the world and the eastern half of Asia (ten countries including China, Hong Kong, Indonesia, Japan, Korea, Malaysia, the Philippines, Singapore, Taiwan Province of China, and Thailand) has grown faster when compared to the rest of the world.

One of the publications which dealt with the issue was the World Bank Report of 1993. World Bank launched a landmark report entitled 'The East Asian Miracle' in September 1993 (World Bank, 1993). This was a controversial report because it credited the economic development witnessed in the four countries viz., Hong Kong, Singapore, South Korea and Taiwan to the neo-liberal policies consisting of export-led growth, low tax regime, minimal welfare state and state intervention. More importantly, the report brought forth the relationship between public policy and rapid economic growth in the context of high economic growth despite wide diversity in natural resources, culture and political institutions.

There were some shared common features in their public policy, including limited price distortion and careful policy interventions. Regardless of the controversy of the causes and the sustainability of the model, there is no denying the fact that these countries underwent rapid industrialization and maintained exceptionally high growth rates (in excess of 7 percent a year) between the early 1960s (mid-1950s for Hong Kong) and 1990s. Their economic success stories have served as role models for many developing countries, especially the Tiger Cub Economies.

The Hong Kong economy was the first out of the four to undergo industrialization with the development of a textile industry in the 1950s. The economy of Hong Kong diversified from textile industry to include clothing, electronics and plastics in the 1960s. In the case of Singapore economy, industrial estates set up during the initial phase of independence became the epicentre of its economic growth. The focus was on attracting foreign investment with tax incentives. Taiwan and South Korea began to industrialize in the mid-1960s with heavy government involvement and both countries pursued export-oriented industrialization as in Hong Kong and Singapore. These four countries had Japan as their role model and as followed in Japan, they invested heavily in education and infrastructure.

There were also foreign trade advantages especially by its closeness to one of the super powers, namely USA. There is no denying the fact that the four countries were influenced by the Confucian ideals of society being more important than individual and the need for group cooperation and sacrifice. By the beginning of the 1970s, these four economies far exceeded other countries in terms of physical and human capital which over a period of time led to rapid growth in per capita income levels. The success of these four countries was to a large extent built on the successful managing of macroeconomic environment. The excellent mechanism of managing budget deficits, external debt and exchange rates along with promoting export policies helped these countries to emerge as leading countries of the region. Some economists argue that state intervention was also instrumental in making these countries grow faster when compared to others in the region (Sarel, 1996). This wave of success in the four countries slowly spread to other countries in Southeast Asia and soon the whole region went on to become successful economically.

Political Economy of Look East Policy

While East Asia and Southeast Asia were making this dramatic progression in economic life of the people, India was struggling economically. Unlike the eastern part of Asia, India's growth rate was low and competitiveness of the economy was strangled by various controls prevalent from the 1970s. Although a major power in South Asia, India was lagging behind many other countries in the region especially China. China had moved on to the road of "open door policy" under Deng Xioping in 1979 and moved rapidly forward in terms of economic growth in a short period.

One of the important aspects which were instrumental with regard to India's economic reforms of 1991 is the success achieved by Southeast Asian countries and China in its journey of economic development. By following a policy which was market driven and focussing on exports, Southeast Asian countries achieved economic transformation. Similar was the case of China and how a socialist country was able to transform itself economically in a short span of time.

There have been dramatic changes in case of India with regard to economic policies, mostly forced by both domestic as well as international factors in the late 1980s and early 1990s. India's balance of payment crisis and subsequent economic liberalization, coupled with the collapse of the USSR and ASEAN's success as a model for regional cooperation in contrast to the stagnated South Asian Association for Regional Cooperation (SAARC), forced a rethink and pulled New Delhi's attention toward Southeast Asia via its 'Look East Policy' under then Indian Prime Minister P.V. Narasimha Rao.

The economic reforms of 1991, and the major global shifts prompted major change, and India's approach toward Southeast Asia not only sought to build on historical links, but also took into account major economic and strategic interests. The immense economic opportunities and the strong historical connectivity in Southeast Asia, as well as a desire by India not to be restricted to South Asia and get bogged down in regional conflicts, were vital. To a large extent, it was driven by real politik as opposed to mere idealism more visible during the 1970 s and 1980s. This policy was named "Look East", and former Prime Minister P.V. Narasimha Rao outlined his vision for Southeast Asia during a speech in Singapore in September 1994.

India and ASEAN

ASEAN came into existence when the war in Indo-china was escalating. The general pro-western orientation of the original five members of ASEAN compelled India to distance itself from ASEAN. The end of Cold War and change in economies around the world due to globalisation ushered in a new phase of rediscovery and renaissance in relationship between India and ASEAN. The 1990s offered a combination of opportunities and challenges for both India and Southeast Asia.

India's 'Look East' and 'Act East Policy' have seen fruitful progress in its association with ASEAN. India's relationship with ASEAN is a key pillar of India's foreign policy and the foundation of the 'Act East Policy'. India and ASEAN relations have progressed steadily over the years. From being Sectorial Dialogue Partner of ASEAN in 1992, India became a full dialogue partner of ASEAN in 1995. In 1996, membership in ASEAN Regional Forum was given to India. The upgradation of the relationship into a Strategic Partnership in 2012 was a natural progression to the ground covered since India Summit Level Partner in 2002. There are, in total, 30 Dialogue Mechanisms between India and ASEAN, cutting across various sectors to deal with diverse issues (MEA, 2017).

Commerce, culture and connectivity are the three pillars of India's robust engagement with ASEAN. In the economic arena, the India-ASEAN relations are poised to scale new frontiers. One of the main indications of the growth in the relationship is the economic synergy between both the regions. None can be more indicative than the increase in trade and investment in recent times. ASEAN is India's fourth largest trading partner. India's trade with ASEAN increased to US$ 70 billion in 2016-17 from US$ 65 billion in 2015-16. India's export to ASEAN increased to US$ 30 billion in 2016-17 from US$ 25 billion in 2015-16 (MEA, 2017).

Investment flows are also substantial both ways, with ASEAN accounting for approximately 12.5 percent of investment flows into India since 2000. FDI inflows into India from ASEAN between April 2000 to May 2016 was about US$ 49.40 billion, while FDI outflows from India to ASEAN countries from April 2007 to March 2015, as per data maintained by DEA, was about US$ 38.672 billion. The ASEAN-India Free Trade Area has been completed with the entering into force of the ASEAN-India Agreements on Trade in Services and Investments on July 1, 2015 (ibid). One of the crucial inputs with regard to sustaining the increase in trade, investment etc. is the private sector involvement.

ASEAN and India has been working on enhancing private sector engagement. With this objective, ASEAN India-Business Council (AIBC) was set up in March 2003 in Kuala Lumpur as a forum to bring key private sector players from India and the ASEAN countries on a single platform for business networking and sharing of ideas. AIBC organizes many business development conclaves. As India and ASEAN observe 25 years of Dialogue Partnership, 15 years of Summit Level interaction and 5 years of Strategic Partnership, one of the main goals of 'Look East' and later 'Act East Policy' has been fulfilled.

Connectivity—physical, institutional and mental—remains the main focus of the India-ASEAN engagement in the Act East concept of Indian foreign policy. India's strategy on this front has been to weave the region together in an intricate web of road, rail and maritime links. This was worked out through a host of transnational projects that seek to connect different regions (Manish Chand, 2014).

One of the achievements on this issue is the completion of the Tamu-Kalewa-Kalemyo sector of the India-Myanmar-Thailand Trilateral Highway. This is poised to create a new dynamic in India's multi-faceted ties with the region and will enable better trade and solve the connectivity lacunae's. With the priority of the Indian government turning towards North-East, and with the renewed vigour on spurring the economic uplift of India's North-Eastern states—the gateway to ASEAN—enhanced connectivity promises to unleash a new prosperity in this region. In the days ahead, enhancing shipping and air connectivity will be the major focus areas.

As a policy enhancing the relationship, India has set up an Indian mission to the ASEAN in Jakarta, and has set up an ASEAN-India Centre in New Delhi. The key areas to be focussed include capacity-building, developmental cooperation, and knowledge partnership. As a means to increase the capacity building, few projects have been taken up in Southeast Asian countries through three funds viz. the US$ 50 million ASEAN-India Cooperation Fund; the US$ 5 million ASEAN-India Green Fund; and the ASEAN-India Science and Technology Fund. Considering India's expertise in information technology (IT), India plans to set up four IT Centres in Cambodia, Lao PDR, Myanmar and Vietnam. India is also set to launch a Tracking and Data Reception Centre in Ho Chi Minh City in Vietnam, which would make remote sensing data available from the RESOURCESAT and OCEANSAT for applications in disaster management and mineral exploration for ASEAN countries (Manish Chand, 2014).

Culture and creativity which existed for centuries can definitely nurture the growing engagement between both the regions. Known in ancient times as Suvarnabhumi, the land of gold, Southeast Asia has deep connections with the Indian culture. Ramayana and Mahabharata go beyond as Indian epics, and are relished as civilizational memories India shares with many Southeast Asian countries like Indonesia, Thailand and Cambodia. Buddhism can be considered as the spiritual nucleus of India-ASEAN relations. Buddhists from all over the region consider India as a sacred land and flock for pilgrimage to revered shrines like Bodh Gaya. One of the important developments has been the establishment of Nalanda University and the support provided many Southeast Asian countries for the same.

India's relations with ASEAN is an example of how nations change when geopolitics come into play on both domestic as well as external front. The loss of five decades in relationship between both the countries has seen an upsurge. There are opportunities and challenges and with the change in attitude of India with regard to 'Look East/Act East Policy', there is a room for transformation between these regions. An example of this change can be understood by certain signals. India invited premiers of all the Southeast Asian nations to be the guest of honour for the Republic Day celebrations in 2018. This one single gesture shows the importance given by India for Southeast Asian nations.

BIMSTEC Initiative

Next stage in the development was the evolution of BIMSTEC. BIST-EC (Bangladesh, India, Sri Lanka, Thailand-Economic Cooperation) was formed at a meeting in June 1997 in Bangkok. Myanmar was admitted in December 1997 and the organization was renamed as BIMST-EC. The grouping expanded when Nepal and Bhutan were admitted in February 2004. The grouping's name was changed to BIMSTEC (Bay of Bengal Initiative for Multi-Sectoral Technical and

Economic Cooperation) at 1st Summit Meeting held in Bangkok in July 2004.

The potential of BIMSTEC is enormous in terms of the potential—a huge market waiting to be tapped. One of the problems India faced with regard to non-functioning of SAARC in terms of its economic potential, because of intra-SAARC political conflicts and fears among the smaller states about losing their economic and political sovereignty to the regional "hegemon" etc. was rectified through this grouping. BIMSTEC is not hostage to any perennial conflict such as the Indo-Pak one. There is also a symbiotic relationship between India and Thailand. BIMSTEC stemmed from India's 'Look East Policy' and Thailand's 'Look West Policy' and through this India can be a part of East Asia's growing economy and also Thailand could gain free access to the growing Indian market.

The BIMSTEC region offers a market of 1.6 billion people, about a fifth of the global population. In 2013, intra-BIMSTEC trade was US$ 74.63 billion, up from US$ 25.16 billion in 2005. The share of India's trade with BIMSTEC remains much below its potential for reasons such as poor connectivity and hurdles in trade facilitation leading to high trade costs, weak supply capabilities especially in least developed countries such as Myanmar, Nepal and Bangladesh. If the BIMSTEC Free Trade Agreement is put in place, trade within BIMSTEC could go up by US$ 43 to US$ 59 billion. But to realize this goal, the woefully inadequate transport and infrastructural facilities in the member countries will have to be enhanced significantly.

One of the crucial inputs which required from converting the Look East to Act East is the need for putting more political capital into sorting out bilateral issues with other BIMSTEC countries, especially Bangladesh and Sri Lanka. In order to move beyond the failures of SAARC, it is important to build bridges with neighbouring countries and to tap on the potential of countries like Myanmar to connect between South and Southeast Asia. It is also important to accommodate Sri Lanka to play a proactive role in and around the Bay of Bengal. There is need to address the connectivity issues of both Nepal and Bhutan which are land-locked and once the issue of connectivity is addressed, trade and investment can be increased too.

Mekong-Ganga Co-operation Initiatives

The Mekong-Ganga Cooperation (MGC) is an initiative by six countries—India and five ASEAN countries, namely, Cambodia, Lao PDR, Myanmar, Thailand and Vietnam for cooperation in tourism, culture, education, as well as transport and communications. It was launched in 2000 at Vientiane, Lao PDR. Both the Ganga and the Mekong are civilizational rivers, and the MGC initiative aims to facilitate closer contacts among the people inhabiting these two major river basins. The MGC is also indicative of the cultural and commercial linkages among the member countries of the MGC down the centuries (MEA, 2017).

Conclusion

The 'Look-East/Act East Policy' is a comprehensive approach not restricted to economic objectives alone. It is much more and strategic importance of the geopolitical location between India and Southeast Asia cannot be minimized. However, the driving force of these relationships is economic and both regions can progress with a win-win situation, if the opportunities are utilized and challenges faced. While intertwining the collective dreams of 1.8 billion people, India and Southeast Asia can expand the arc of prosperity across the region and script a new narrative of an Asian renaissance if the potentials of 'Look East/Act East' policies are fulfilled through systematic policies. To a large extent the first step has been taken by policy makers in both the regions sensing the changed scenario. As the journey of thousand miles start with a single step, it is hoped that both India and Southeast Asia are on the road to make 21st century as the Asian century.

References

Acharya, Amitav (2009), "Constructing a Security Community in Southeast Asia: ASEAN and the Problem of Regional Order", Routledge: New Delhi.

Anand, Mohit (2009), "India-ASEAN Relations: Analyzing Regional Implications", Institute of Peace and Conflict Studies, IPCS Special Report No. 72, May.

Carbaugh, R.J. (2008), "International Economics", Cengage Learning India Limited: New Delhi.

Chand, Manish (2014), "Act East: India's ASEAN Journey", *AJPS*, November 10.

Frost, Ellen I. (2009), "India's Role in East Asia: Lessons from Cultural and Historical Linkages", RIS Discussion Paper, January, pp. 4-5.

Martin, Jacques (2012), "When China Rules the World: The End of the Western World and the Birth of a New Global Order", 2nd edition, Penguin: New York.

Mishra, S.N. (1994), "India: The Cold War Years", South Asian Publishers Pvt. Ltd.: New Delhi, p. 164.

Sarel, Michael (1996), "Growth in East Asia; What We Can and What We Cannot Infer", International Monetary Fund, September.

Sikri, Rajiv (2009), "India's Look East Policy", *Asia-Pacific Review*, Vol. 16, Issue 1.

Suriyanarayan, V. (1996), "India and the Southeast Asia in 1990s: New Perspective and New Challenges", in Baladas Ghoshal (ed.), 'India and Southeast Asia: Challenges and Opportunities', Konark Publishers: New Delhi, p. 18.

World Bank (1993), "The East Asian Miracle: Economic Growth and Public Policy", World Bank Publications.

3

Act East Policy and the Relevance of the QUAD

Muraleedharan Nair

Introduction

The official level talks on expanding cooperation and security coordination in the Indo-Pacific region by Australia, India, Japan and the United States held on the sidelines of the ASEAN and East Asia Summits in Manila on November 12, 2017 signalled the 're-birth' of the Quadrilateral Security Dialogue Mechanism (QUAD). The Chinese allegations that these nations were 'ganging up to contain' [1], was promptly dismissed. However, there is no denying the fact that it is the increased assertive and often aggressive Chinese policies that have been playing out in the Indo-Pacific region, and particularly in the South China Sea in recent years, that triggered a sense of urgency in the QUAD participants to come together for a second time to protect their common interests in this strategically important region, 'a new engine of prosperity'. [2]

China's Assertiveness

The rise of China, especially its asymmetric militarization has been a cause of worry for the world in general and the region in particular. The Southeast Asian nations started feeling the heat as China's aggressive land grab policy in the South China Sea had a direct impact on their territorial claims and right to exploit natural resources in the disputed territories. Their freedom of navigation in the region appeared to be under increased threat. At the same time, India was getting increasingly uncomfortable with similar developments closer home. The boundary dispute between India and China assumed new patterns of intimidation.

There cannot be any argument on the assertion that the South China Sea includes "the most strategically important maritime territory on earth". [3] Nor can there be a dispute on its vital strategic significance for China. According to some studies, there are 11 billion barrels of oil and 190 trillion cubic feet of natural gas in deposits under the sea, quite substantial quantities by any estimates. This heavily fished sea contains more than 10 percent of the global seafood resources. Nearly 40 percent of China's seaborne trade (worth about US$ 1,470 billion) passes through South China Sea. About 80 percent of its crude oil imports and two-thirds of its LNG imports reach the country through this sea. China, therefore, considers control of the sea vital to its economic survival. At the same time, according to a 2015 study, US$ 5.3 trillion worth of global seaborne trade, i.e., about a third of global maritime trade, passes through the sea annually. About 50 percent of India's trade, 60 percent of Japan's energy supplies, and two-thirds of the South Korean energy resources also pass through the region. [4]

Therefore, like China, for the US, Japan, South Korea, India, the ASEAN countries, and a host of others as well, South China Sea is a critical transit route for their trade and energy supplies, and therefore, its significance to them. China now claims about 90 percent of the South China Sea by producing a controversial Nine-Dash Line 1947 vintage map which the then KMT government had unilaterally drawn post-World War II Japanese surrender. [5] The Chinese claim has not been accepted by any other claimant littoral states, particularly Vietnam, the Philippines, Indonesia and Brunei. The Nine-Dash Lines gobbles up roughly 80,000 sq. km. of territories running right inside the exclusive economic zones (EEZs) of some coastal states, as also areas hitherto treated as international waters. The nearest Chinese mainland coast is hundreds of kilometres away from some of the islands it claims, and its EEZ, if calculated from the mainland coast, does not overlap the EEZs of other claimant countries. China, in its quest for strategic control of the sea, even prevents the smaller coastal nations from exploiting the marine wealth traditionally availed of by them, or the fisher folks of both the sides or even by outsiders in some cases.

Showing total disregard to the territorial claims of other littoral states, China developed reefs, cays, low-tide elevations, shoals and submerged features and other outcrops into small islands and constructed helipads, POL dumps, lighthouses, radar domes, multi-storey buildings, wind turbines, observation and communication towers and even airfields and hangars, claiming that it was for tourism purposes. [6] It even brought in several batches of mainland 'tourists' for some time, before militarising the islands. China harassing Vietnamese, Philippino and Indonesian vessels in the disputed waters became a common feature. It prevented Vietnam particularly in its oil exploration efforts, some of which jointly were developed with India's ONGC Videsh Ltd. [7]

The tactics adopted to disrupt the Vietnamese efforts included frequently moving around its own oil rigs and related offshore platforms in the Vietnam-claimed areas, and threatening international oil majors involved in Vietnamese projects with strong retaliatory measures. The frequent face offs, shoving and ramming by apparently civilian vessels involving China and other claimant countries helped only in further straining the mutual trust. The then Chinese Foreign Minister, later State Councillor Yang Jiechi's angry outburst at the 2010 Hanoi ASEAN Regional Forum, staring down at the then Singaporean Foreign Minister George Yeo that "China is a big country and other countries are small countries, and that's just a fact", that too after mocking at the host nation Vietnam, was one of the most open exhibitions of Chinese insolence (that too, by a senior leader) towards its smaller ASEAN neighbours. [8]

The hurt such actions created in the ASEAN psyche was palpable, but the ASEAN members in general do not have the tenacity to stand up to the Chinese brazenness. If India is blamed for not participating in the Belt and Road Initiative conference in Beijing in May 2017, the absence of the Singaporean Prime Minister Lee Hsien Loong and Thai Prime Minister Gen. Prayut Chan-o-cha was also noticed, especially as these two countries are prominent points in the maritime Silk Road alignment. [9]

A pattern emerged when away from the South China Sea, China unilaterally declared an Air Defence Identification Zone (ADIZ) over East China Sea in November 2013 that covers an area over Diaoyu Islands (Senkaku in Japanese). [10] Though claimed by China, the islands are administered by Japan. Besides adding another irritant to the already sensitive Sino-Japanese relations, the move elicited strong opposition from Korea and the US as well. The East China Sea also witnessed its own share of 'pushing, shoving and ramming' episodes involving ostensibly Chinese civilian fishing trawlers and Japanese vessels, including the vessels of the latter's Coast Guard and MSDF [navy]. There were incidents of radar locking and even spraying of paint using fire hydrants on a Japan MSDF vessel. [11]

There have also been instances of Chinese naval vessels sailing just off the Okinawan coast and PLAN helicopters flying dangerously close to Japan's MSDF ships, though in international waters. China has, on more than one occasion, cut off shipments of rare earth to Japan, an important input for its electronics industry, to coerce Japan to agree to the Chinese arguments. Incidentally, the pattern is familiar to any China watcher who has been observing the ongoing incidents of 'pushing and shoving'—the Chinese soldiers engaged with their Indian counterparts along the 'Indian side' of the Line of Actual Control. Quite naturally, China's aggressive activities in the Indo-Pacific made other stakeholders like Australia and the United States also worried about the former's long-term motives.

India, QUAD and ASEAN

The presence of all the ten ASEAN heads of state/government in New Delhi at the Commemorative Summit with the theme, 'Shared Values, Common Destiny' on January 25, 2018 and the next day as chief guests at the 69th Republic Day Parade was generally viewed as "an unprecedented gesture of goodwill" from the ASEAN nations that portrayed a remarkable show of India-ASEAN solidarity. But, are all the ASEAN nations strong enough to stand up to the Chinese assertiveness alongside the QUAD? At the Commemorative Summit and official level meetings, there was reiteration of the need for a rules-based maritime order, freedom of navigation etc. in South China Sea, which according to India will "enhance [the] shared maritime domain". [12]

There was also mention of "the need for peaceful resolution of dispute in accordance with UNCLOS and standards of the International Civil Aviation Organisation and International Maritime Organisation". Prime Minister Narendra Modi stressed on the importance of "ASEAN-India cooperation in the maritime domain as one of the key focus areas for growth and development for the Indo-Pacific region". [13]

But, the response from ASEAN leaders in their media interactions was rather subdued. The fact is that though there is a deep wariness in ASEAN against the Chinese assertiveness in the South China Sea, ASEAN members, with few exceptions, are generally careful not to speak against China in the open, particularly in multilateral forums. They are aware that any reference to freedom of navigation and respect for law [read UNCLOS] is interpreted as a diplomatic snub by China. Notably, Indonesian President Joko Widodo, who took a much publicised naval ship ride to disputed areas had, at the New Delhi Commemorative Summit, expressed "the desire for more deliberations by key players to discuss the concept of Indo-Pacific"! [14]

It may be recalled that the Philippines, under the then President Benigno Aquino, had rallied ASEAN in criticising

China for its aggressive moves in the South China Sea. Its campaign culminated in the country taking China to the Permanent Court of Arbitration in The Hague in 2013. [That China took the stand that the Court had no jurisdiction to hear the Philippine claim and promptly rejected its ruling (that has wider ramifications with regard to similar disputes with Vietnam, Indonesia and Brunei) is yet another example of China's impudence.] [15] When Rodrigo Duterte took over as the president of the Philippines in June 2016, followed by the country becoming the chair of the ASEAN for 2017, its approach to the South China Sea dispute vis-à-vis China changed dramatically.

The section on the South China Sea in the chair's statement simply "took note of concerns expressed by some leaders over recent developments in the area". [16] It did not even mention about their "concerns" and instead watered it down to taking "note of the improving relations between ASEAN and China". While no one could understand what "improvement" was being talked about, it was quite obvious that President Duterte was won over by China's alluring economic diplomacy. In fact, it is not only the Philippines, but there are other ASEAN members like Lao DPR or even Cambodia that have fallen for China's largesse.

Though there are exceptions like Vietnam, and perhaps Singapore, a non-claimant nation, can the ASEAN's wholehearted support for a Quadrilateral effort to realise a rules-based system in the South China Sea be taken for granted? In my view, having accomplished what it wanted in the first phase of aggressive strategic land grabbing in the South China Sea, China would try and stitch together *bilateral* agreements on the South China Sea dispute with say, claimant states like the Philippines and Brunei and non-claimant ASEAN members like Lao DPR or Cambodia, making it a non-ASEAN issue. China would, thus, try and consolidate its position and make sure that no other claimant country engages in militarization of disputed outcrops and ensures that its strategic upper hand in South China Sea remains in place for a very long time to come.

It is another matter that not many claimant ASEAN nations presently have the wherewithal to develop the reefs, shoals etc. in the disputed waters and convert them into military outposts the way China did in the past years.

Common Interests, Shared Responsibility

For the stakeholders in the Indo-Pacific, there is an urgent need to establish a "rules-based security architecture that attests to the region's interests and its peaceful development". [17] In other words, those countries in the Indo-Pacific region that are not willing to submit to a China-led regional order are left with no option but to come together and impress upon China to follow "a rules-based international order where nobody is big winner or a big loser, and every country is a winner on its own right". [18] The founding of Quadrilateral Security Dialogue mechanism involving Australia, India, Japan and the United States was, thus, participating in a new geo-strategic architecture to share responsibility for protecting the common interests.

As discussed elsewhere, for India, the maintenance of peace and tranquillity in the Indo-Pacific, and particularly in the South China Sea, is central to the success of its 'Look East', now 'Act East Policy', and hence the need for participating in this new geo-strategic architecture. The formation of QUAD would have also soothed some nerves in the Indian security circles worried with the Chinese String of Pearls conundrum for some time now.

China's Response

Even as the South China Sea land grab was happening, China has also been engaged in building deep sea commercial ports with the potential to turn them into naval outposts at short notice at strategic locations, including in India's close neighbourhood, like the one at Hambantota in Sri Lanka. The establishment of its first overseas naval base in Djibouti, and the reported plans to have another naval outpost at Jiwani near Gwadar, or at Gwadar itself in Pakistan, reveal China's real long-term plans for the region.

According to reports, including those in the government-controlled Chinese media, but subsequently denied by the government, Beijing has plans to establish about eighteen 'overseas strategic support bases' in important locations, like Sonadia Islands (Bangladesh), Maldives, Myanmar, Aden, Salalah, Seychelles, Yemen, Oman, Kenya, Tanzania, Mozambique, Seychelles and Madagascar in the Indian Ocean and Walvis Bay (Namibia), along the South Atlantic coast. In other words, after securing what it wanted in the South China Sea, and taking requisite steps in South Asia, it is moving fast in the larger Indo-Pacific region, right up to the Horn of Africa and even beyond. [19] Incidentally, when the world has since adopted the term 'Indo-Pacific', for China it is still 'Asia-Pacific', particularly in all its diplomatic discourses.

With an enormous money chest with hardly any public auditing at its disposal, and a matching capacity to deliver on promises with precision, China has done well for itself abroad in the past decade or more. In the 19th National Congress of Chinese Communist Party held in October 2017, President Xi Jinping emphasised on "striving for achievement" and "the construction of a community of common destiny" as two of China's guiding foreign policy concepts for the future. [20] In his keynote speech at the 13th National People's Congress held in March 2018, President Xi asserted that not an inch of Chinese territory will be allowed to be separated [from the country] under any circumstance. [21]

From these statements, and among other indications like the [current] Foreign Minister promoted as State Councillor, it is clear that the country will navigate the same course of increased strategic engagement overseas in the near and midterm as well. This would mean that its policies for the Indo-Pacific in general, and South Asia and Southeast Asia in particular would continue without any major changes. In other words, the country is going to push ahead with the asymmetric military build-up, which it feels is absolutely essential to protect its emerging pre-eminence in the world, including for the safety and security of its seaborne trade, energy supplies and overseas Belt and Road Initiative projects. The Chinese portrayal of itself as a developing country and friend of the third world is passé now. Whether it admits openly or not, today's China enjoys basking in the halo of intermittent [Chinese] media projection of it as a member of 'G-2' [alongside the US], a position it believes, and it is deservingly entitled to. [22] In other words, the days of China's much touted *peaceful rise* are long over.

The first Chinese reaction to the announcement of the Manila QUAD meeting was on expected lines, with the Chinese media playing the victim of a 'sinister move' by the so-called democracies, "ganging up to contain China's rise". [23] But they hastened to assert that China cannot be contained. The official Chinese reaction was not much different from that of the government/Communist Party-controlled media. Quoting a Chinese proverb, the official Chinese reaction then turned harsher to threaten that "when you want to create an enemy, there is one ready". China has always been uneasy when any of its neighbours got closer to India or Japan, or when the latter two moved closer to each other. New Delhi or Tokyo getting close to Washington DC is another major cause of annoyance to Beijing, as has been evident from the [government-guided] Chinese media hyperbole during such past developments.

However, five days after the announcement of the Quad meeting, Chinese Ambassador to India Luo Zhaohui repeated at a Jawaharlal Nehru University (JNU) event an earlier suggestion [at United Services Institution in New Delhi on May 5, 2018] that his country was willing to consider changing the name and alignment of the China-Pakistan Economic Corridor if India agreed to join the Belt and Road

Initiative. [24] He added that one of his goals was to conclude a bilateral trade and friendship treaty with New Delhi during his tenure in the country. Clearly, he would not have made such an unusual comment for a Chinese Ambassador to India without the approval or instructions from Beijing. However, it is yet to be verified whether his statement at JNU was in response to the formation of the QUAD, a subject that had also come up for discussion at the event. The Chinese reaction has, thus, been strong, but typically ambivalent at times.

India, among others, played down the development, and clarified that containing China was not on the QUAD's agenda. [25] Even a cursory look at modern history would show that efforts by a nation or a group of nations to 'contain' another have not succeeded for various reasons. In a modern, connected world that works on a globalised trade and commercial format, any move to 'contain' an economic superpower like China is doomed to fail. The usage 'containing China' is, thus, clear hyperbole. It was further explained that what the QUAD nations seek is a China that sheds its disdain for a rules-based system and its aggressive approach to settling disputes.

It is apparent that these nations believe that if China is not persuaded into respecting international norms, including in matters like freedom of navigation and over flight and peaceful resolution of disputes sooner, it might be difficult to convince Beijing on such matters later when it gains even more economic heft and military muscle. Will the QUAD succeed in driving home its message that China needs to respect a rules-based order in the Indo-Pacific, particularly with regard to its aggressive behaviour born partly out of the middle kingdom-attitude, in South and East China Seas? The answer is straight and simple: it is too early to draw a conclusion on this as a lot will depend on the shape and structure the QUAD is going to take, and how effective and forceful the pressure it would be able to put on China in this regard. The key words to watch for in this context are the ones attributed to Xi Jinping at the 19th Party Congress: *"the construction of a community of common destiny"*. [26] At the same time, the Belt and Road Initiative, could be China's long-term response to the QUAD formation.

QUAD and India's Strategic Autonomy

As already discussed, even as the QUAD meeting attracted wide global attention, the fact that should not be glossed over is that a trilateral dialogue with the US, Japan and India with the focus on Indo-Pacific has been in place at the official level. The dialogue was upgraded to the Foreign Minister-level on the sidelines of the UNGA session in 2015. The first ever Trilateral Summit of the heads of the three governments was held in November 2018. This was followed by the second Trilateral Summit meeting on the margins of the G20 Osaka Summit on June 28, 2019. [27] Secondly, a Foreign Secretary-level trilateral with India, Japan and Australia to guarantee an "open and free Indo-Pacific" that began in June 2015 has also been happening since then. [28] It would be interesting to see the future role of both these trilateral dialogue mechanisms following the revival of the Quadrilateral Security Dialogue Mechanism—for the main focus of each of these three initiatives is also Indo-Pacific.

In such a scenario, it is time that the QUAD declared its aims and objectives, its possible structure and the role it hopes to play in different areas other than ensuring a rules-based system in the Indo-Pacific. New Zealand, among others, has already raised the issue in recent separate interactions with the QUAD members. How will the QUAD strategise countering Chinese manipulations in the region, like bolstering un-democratic regimes in the region, as witnessed in the case of Abdulla Yameen in the Maldives? While China exhorts the principle of non-interference in internal political developments in smaller countries, it actually continues with its strategy of cleverly installing amenable regimes, like it did from behind the scenes in Nepal.

How the QUAD is planning to operate in areas like natural disasters, man-made pollution, piracy, seaborne terrorism etc.?

Will the QUAD take interest in solving regional political and economic disputes involving its members and others? Will the QUAD seek China's active cooperation in such matters if the group's aim is not to 'contain' it, as the country alleges? Is the QUAD going to take the shape of a military alliance in future or will it in the least have a military component to help achieve its objectives? Does it propose to coordinate its activities with any other powers in Europe, say France for example, or New Zealand in South-Western Pacific or some amenable countries in the Middle East and the African east coast? And most importantly, what concessions in terms of controversial issues like navigational rights in the Indo-Pacific, and particularly in the Indian Ocean, QUAD is willing to negotiate with China as quid pro quo for reaching understanding on various disputes?

QUAD should clarify such issues, or at least whatever is possible at this stage, and take into confidence as many countries in the region as possible to pre-empt the earlier mentioned Chinese countermove in this regard.

With the QUAD coming into existence, is India going to shed its long-cherished strategic autonomy in foreign policy? Is the country finally walking into the US camp as alleged in the Chinese media and in certain quarters in India itself? It is common knowledge that President Donald Trump has little interest in sharing strategic responsibilities overseas, or propagating and protecting democratic values abroad, ideals the US kept close to its heart for a long time. While there may not have been any major shift in the US policy of Rebalance to Asia over the years, the US leadership did create confusion about its strategic commitment to the region even during the second Obama administration.

In fact, the US strategy had begun stressing on creating smaller alliances or partnerships in different regions of importance to pursue its regional strategic interests. Donald Trump is also keen that regional allies and friends "pay for the security cover" they enjoy, or build their own stronger militaries, and buy expensive weapon systems [from the US, of course] for the purpose. [29] If the major stakeholders came forward to share the US's perceived 'overburden' in fulfilling multilateral commitments in the Indo-Pacific, it would be an incentive for the US to stay put in the region.

The QUAD may, thus, be viewed as an upgraded version of the US policy of Rebalance in Asia. But the convergence of its core interests with those of India's 'Act East Policy' and Japan's "reinvigorated role as a pro-active contributor to peace" is too tangible to be ignored. [30] In other words, viewed against the background of China's assertiveness in the region, the continued presence of the US in the Indo-Pacific as a balancer, in the QUAD or otherwise, is vital for maintaining a rules-based system in the region. As discussed at the beginning, it is also critical for the long-term success of India's 'Act East Policy'.

If QUAD is going to have a cooperative strategic/military architecture, the possibility of India, a country that so determinedly desisted from joining any formal military alliance since Independence, fighting a war that is thrust upon it indirectly, cannot be ruled out. That would be the first time the country would be engaging in a war that is not for protecting its borders. (The brief intervention in the Maldives in 1988 and the peacekeeping mission that turned sour in Sri Lanka (1987-1990), both on behalf and at the explicit request of the elected regimes in those countries is a different story). In other words, in case of a military confrontation involving a QUAD member with China in the South China Sea or somewhere farther away in the Indo-Pacific, it would be binding on India to get involved in it.

In such an eventuality, the country should be ready to handle a spill over of the development at its long, unsettled land border with China. Whether or not Pakistan gets involved in it in some way or the other at China's bidding, India should be prepared for such an eventuality in its western borders as well. Among the QUAD members, India's geopolitical location is unique as it is the only member state that shares a land border with China.

The strategic potential of the QUAD had played out in an accidental stroke of history in the aftermath of the tsunami that hit the Indo-Pacific region in December 2004. In a spontaneous coordinated effort, the navies of India, the US, Japan and Australia launched a massive rescue, relief and rehabilitation mission before its leadership was handed over to the UN later in mid-January 2005. Even as the Indian coast was also badly affected, Indian naval vessels on rescue and relief mission reached the Sri Lankan coast and the Maldivian atolls within hours. Secondly, with Japan participating in the India-US joint naval Exercise Malabar, [31] and Australia likely to join it sooner than later, the strategic arm of QUAD may be said to have been primed.

Other nations from the region, viz., Vietnam, Indonesia, or perhaps the Philippines under a new regime, who feel the heat of the "Chinese expansionist brazenness" might decide to associate with the mechanism at a later stage in some form or the other. Then, some non-member nations, Singapore or Malaysia for example, who might not wish to assign their offshore platforms for operational activities, could chip in and allow QUAD to use their onshore logistical facilities. Further, some QUAD members including India have agreements and understandings between themselves, as also with Indian Ocean littoral states for using each other's naval facilities. India also has similar agreements with 'outside forces' like France. Whether or not all of them would agree to permit the QUAD to use their facilities in a real-time war situation is another matter. On the whole, the picture of the QUAD that is currently emerging is that of a benign, but potent Indo-Pacific force that China would have to reckon with.

Differences within QUAD

Though the move to formally set up a Quadrilateral Security Dialogue Mechanism took off at the initiative of the then Japanese Prime Minister Shinzo Abe way back in 2007, and the blame for its early deep-freezing is dumped at the doorsteps of an allegedly China-friendly Australian Prime Minister Kevin Rudd for his fear of antagonising that country, the US also cannot be absolved of its role in 'cold-storaging' the idea then. The US felt that annoying China at the time would come in the way its efforts to, among other things, get Chinese support for the Iran deal and the North Korean talks, and eventually for getting the North Korean sanctions widened. As for Australia, a country that depends heavily on China for its resources exports and investments, the question is will it do a Kevin Rudd again and backtrack on its commitments to the QUAD in the future?

As mentioned above, it was Australia that was chosen by China this time for a formal 'dressing down' for the revival of the QUAD security dialogue mechanism. [32] Will Japan soften its current stand vis-à-vis China if it assesses in the future that it can achieve its goals by mending its relations with that country? Will the trilateral dialogue mechanism between Japan, China and South Korea, convened in May 2018 after a two-year hiatus, produce good results in the *long- term*, consequently reducing Tokyo's commitment to the QUAD? [33] Will China succeed in buying the silence of more ASEAN members through its well-known economic diplomacy, an indication of which was witnessed at the Manila Summit? Will the US repeat 2007, not only for China's help vis-à-vis Iran and North Korea this time, but also for getting economic and trade concessions from the Chinese?

For example, during his 5-nation November 2017 Asia tour in general, and his engagements in Beijing in particular, President Donald Trump seemed interested mostly, if not only, in his America First doctrine and squeezing concessions out of China, rather than anything else, including the South China Sea dispute. Even as he kept asking the Asian leaders to put pressure on North Korea on nuclear and missile issues, he was clearly silent on South China Sea. Understandably, Japan has also been carefully avoiding making a big issue out of the sensitive South China and East China Sea disputes at the ASEAN+ Three meetings involving heads of governments of ASEAN and China, Japan and South Korea.

Though the India-ASEAN relationship has been improving steadily, there are issues that await resolution. For example, the difficulties in concluding Regional Comprehensive Economic Partnership (RCEP) agreement that has the potential to create the largest free trade zone in the world. India maintains that there should be a balance between the three pillars of RCEP, viz., goods, services and investments. While ASEAN is pushing for tariff-related concessions on trade alleging that India's stance on it was 'stalling' the process, India blames that the former is not amenable particularly to India's demands for concessions in the services sector and free flow of human resources. [34] India is also worried about China flooding the Indian markets with various types of products that has the potential to further damage the domestic industry.

Apart from that, there is unhappiness in ASEAN about India's incapability in delivering on promises due to, among other things, liquidity issues. For example, though the decision to build the 1,360 kilometres long trilateral highway from Moreh in Manipur to Mae Sot in Thailand, through Bagan in Myanmar, was taken way back in April 2001, the completion of the project had to be rescheduled on more than one occasion for various reasons. India was also blamed in the past for "dragging its feet" on taking a decision on its extension to Cambodia and Lao PDR and for a new highway in Vietnam. How fast and how well would India be able to process the ASEAN demands on improving air and maritime links remains to be seen. After all, an FTA becomes meaningless without combining it with other important essentials like reducing transport costs by improving connectivity links. On the contrary, for China to raise its share of the US$ 3 billion for the China-ASEAN Investment Cooperation Fund (CAF) for investments under the 'Belt and Road Initiative' in Southeast Asia, was a cakewalk. [35]

There are similarities in interests between India's 'Act East Policy' and the US policy on Rebalance to Asia and Japan's 'reinvigorated role as a pro-active contributor to peace'. However, these similarities do not necessarily reflect in their views on other multilateral issues, like those related to climate change or the WTO. In fact, India's views on several such matters are more similar to that of China than to that of the US. Differences also exist between India and the US on issues like the rights of foreign naval vessels in the exclusive economic zones of the coastal states.

India-China and the QUAD

A natural corollary to India's joining QUAD is that China would try and make things increasingly difficult for it [India] in various bilateral, regional and international platforms. After all, some in China consider India a "weak target" among the foursome. [36] China is likely to continue to maintain a tough stance against India in matters like India's membership to the Nuclear Suppliers Group, India's inclusion in an expanded UN Security Council as a Permanent Member, or on issues like the listing of Pakistan-based terrorist organisations and individuals at the UN. China's annoyance will also be reflected in steps taken in resolving lingering bilateral issues. China's engagements with the smaller neighbours of India would also increase. That all these China is already doing is another matter.

A question being asked in some circles following the QUAD dialogue in Manila is this: Is India ready yet to play the role of a 'net security provider' in the Indo-Pacific? [37] Some observers wonder whether India was "needling China unnecessarily, adding another avoidable irritant" to the already long list [of such issues]? [38] Isn't it wiser for India to use its good offices and the image of a benign power it has in Southeast Asia to play the more appealing role of a 'consensus builder'? As a country that has not been able to resolve decades-long border disputes with both its bigger neighbours, does India possess the moral standing to negotiate with China on the larger issues of South China Sea and the Indo-Pacific, others ask? Will its role as a significant player of QUAD help it in resolving lingering bilateral issues with China? The suggestion in such quarters is for bandwagoning or co-binding with China for resolving bilateral and regional issues.

Viewed against China's attitude towards India on the global scene and its increasingly assertive postures in the Indo-Pacific, suggestions of bandwagoning or co-binding might look vastly ideal, but, in my opinion, only in well-intentioned academic exercises like this. At the same time, what is to be kept in mind is that when it comes to resolving important issues involving a grouping, the Chinese prefer to deal with the member countries individually, as they shun the idea of dealing with blocs per se. A matured country that India is, it must continue to strengthen the current trend of increased all around engagement with China, the country's largest neighboured biggest trading partner with a still unsettled land border. Needless to mention that such engagement should be in the security area as well.

In other words, now that India has finally decided to leave the bench and don the mantle of an active team player, it would do well to engage China both at the bilateral and multilateral levels. By adopting such a two-pronged approach, India would not get caught in a Chinese offside trap, if one or more QUAD teammates decide to repeat a Kevin Rudd at a later stage. India and China must always remember that when two nations rise simultaneously, engaged in resource hunting, expanding markets and securing connectivity links, it is natural that their points of interest overlap. Competition ensues, and it can turn into disputes, especially if the competing countries are neighbours. But statesmanship at the top level can ensure that disputes do not lead to conflicts.

Notes and References

1. Various media reports quoting Chinese Ministry of Foreign Affairs (MOFA).
2. As observed by various leaders and analysts while referring to the region, particularly after the usage 'Indo-Pacific' became popular.
3. The area is referred to as such in a host of articles, reports etc., including in The South China Sea: Explaining the Dispute by Max Fisher, *New York Times*, July 14, 2016.
4. Based on host of studies and assessment by various organisations, available at:

https://amti.csis.org/south-china-sea-energy-exploration-and-development/;https://www.forbes.com/sites/timdaiss/2016/05/22/why-the-south-china-sea-has-more-oil-than-you-think/#d802a73dd8fc;https://www.cnbc.com/2016/10/21/china-and-the-philippines-could-ink-oil-exploration-deal-in-south-china-sea.html;https://www.voanews.com/east-asia-pacific/oil-becoming-code-sovereignty-contested-south-china-sea.

5. Featured in a number of studies and reports, including "The U.S. and China's Nine-Dash Line: Ending the Ambiguity" by Jeffrey A. Bader in Brookings website, February 6, 2014, available at: https://www.brookings.edu/opinions/the-u-s-and-chinas-nine-dash-line-ending-the-ambiguity;
"What Does the Nine-Dash Line Actually Mean?", by Marina Tsirbas in *The Diplomat*, June 2, 2016, available at: https://thediplomat.com/2016/06/what-does-the-nine-dash-line-actually-mean;
"What's China's Nine-Dash Line and Why Has it Created so Much Tension in the South China Sea?", by Liu Zhen, *South China Morning Post*, July 12, 2016.
6. Xiao Jie, the Mayor of what China calls Sansha city, in an interview to *China Daily* as reported *in The Guardian*, May 27, 2016; "Tourists Visit South China Sea Islands as Part of Plan to Develop Disputed Region", by Zhang Yiqian, *Global Times*, April 7, 2016; "Chinese Tourists Hold Flag-raising Ceremony on Disputed Island in South China Sea", by Laurie Chen, *South China Morning Post*, November 19, 2018.
7. "Vietnam Extends Oil Exploration Deal with Indian Firm in South China Sea", by Arun Mathew in *DEFPOST*, July 6, 2017, available at:
https://defpost.com/vietnam-extends-oil-exploration-deal-indian-firm-south-china-sea/;
"India Says ONGC Videsh Will Return South China Sea Block", *Dow Jones Newswires*, Rakesh Sharma, *Rigzone*, May 15, 2012, available at:
https://www.rigzone.com/news/oil_gas/a/117870/india_says_ongc_videsh_will_return_south_china_sea_block.
8. A host of news reports at the time, and speech at Sasakawa Peace Foundation and the Royal United Services Institute, October 1, 2013, available at:
https://www.spf.org/news/dbfiles/47278daadc0.pdf;

"China's 'Frown Diplomacy' in Southeast Asia", East Asia Forum, October 8, 2010, available at: https://www.eastasiaforum.org/2010/10/08/chinas-frown-diplomacy-in-southeast-asia.

9. News reports at the time, and "Why was Thailand's Prime Minister Absent in the Belt and Road Initiative Summit?", by Pongphisoot Busbaratat, ISEAS Yusof Ishak Institute website, June 9, 2017, available at: https://www.iseas.edu.sg/medias/commentaries/item/5557-why-was-thailands-prime-minister-absent-in-the-belt-and-road-initiative-summit-by-pongphisoot-busbarat; "How China Snubbed Singapore at the Belt and Road Summit", by Angelina Han, Lowy Institute website, available at: https://www.lowyinstitute.org/the-interpreter/how-china-snubbed-Singapore-belt-and-road-summit.
10. Media reports, and "China's ADIZ over the East China Sea: A Great Wall in the Sky?" by Jun Osawa, Brookings website, December 17, 2013, available at: https://www.brookings.edu/opinions/chinas-adiz-over-the-east-china-sea-a-great-wall-in-the-sky/; "China Imposes Restrictions on Air Space Over Senkaku Islands", by Zachary Keck, The Diplomat website, November 23, 2013, available at: https://thediplomat.com/2013/11/china-imposes-restrictions-on-air-space-over-senkaku-islands.
11. Japanese Defence Minister Itsunori Onodera's statements carried by media, and "China 'locks radar' on Japanese Navy Vessel and Helicopter as Island Dispute Intensifies", *National Post*, available at: https://nationalpost.com/news/japan-accuses-chinese-navy-vessels-of-using-weapons-radar-on-ship-and-helicopter-as-territorial-dispute-intensifies; "China DM Refutes Japan's Allegations on Radar Targeting" by Xinhua on China Daily website, available at: http://www.chinadaily.com.cn/china/2013-02/08/content_16216914.htm.
12. "India, ASEAN to Step Up Maritime Cooperation" by Elizabeth Roche, *Live Mint*, available at:

https://www.livemint.com/Politics/1WNQ211sLVi4wVSnmh8ghO/India-Asean-to-work-towards-enhancing-trade-Narendra-Modi.html.

13. "While Agreeing on Maritime Cooperation, ASEAN Leaders Prod India on Moving Forward With RCEP", *The Wire,* available at: https://thewire.in/diplomacy/asean-india-summit-rcep-maritime-cooperation.
14. "President Joko Widodo Wants ASEAN-India Partnership Create Indo-Pacific Region Stability" by Ani Hasanah, *RRI News, Voice of Indonesia,* January 26, 2018, available at: http://voinews.id/index.php/component/k2/item/353-president-joko-widodo-wants-asean-india-partnership-create-indo-pacific-region-stability.
15. "Beijing Rejects Tribunal's Ruling in South China Sea Case", *The Guardian,* July 12, 2016, available at: https://www.theguardian.com/world/2016/jul/12/philippines-wins-south-china-sea-case-against-china.
16. "Philippines' Duterte Gives China Free Pass Over Sea Row", April 30, 2017, *The Peninsula,* available at: https://thepeninsulaqatar.com/article/30/04/2017/Philippines-Duterte-gives-China-free-pass-over-sea-row.
17. "South China Sea Row: India Supports Rules-Based Security Architecture, Says PM Modi", *NDTV,* November 14, 2017, available at: https://www.ndtv.com/india-news/south-china-sea-row-india-supports-rules-based-security-architecture-says-pm-modi-1775455.
18. "India, Japan, U.S., Australia Hold First 'Quad' Talks at Manila Ahead of ASEAN Summit", *The Hindu,* November 12-13, 2017, available at: https://www.thehindu.com/news/national/india-highlights-indo-pacific-cooperation-at-the-first-quad-talks/article20317526.ece.
19. "China Denies Reports to Set Up 18 Naval Bases in Indian Ocean", *The Economic Times,* November 27, 2014, available at: https://economictimes.indiatimes.com/news/politics-and-nation/china-denies-reports-to-set-up-18-naval-bases-in-indian-ocean/articleshow/45297247.cms.
20. "The 'Community of Common Destiny' in Xi Jinping's New Era", by Jacob Mardell, *The Diplomat,* October 25, 2017, available at: https://thediplomat.com/2017/10/the-community-of-common-destiny-in-xi-jinpings-new-era.

21. Media reports, including *CGTN* website, March 20, 2018, available at:
https://news.cgtn.com/news/35416a4e7a6b7a6333566d54/share_p.html.
22. "China and the United States: A G2 Within the G20", by Robert Kahn and Steven A. Tananbaum, *Global Economics Monthly,* April 2016, available at:
https://www.cfr.org/sites/default/files/pdf/2016/04/GEM%20April%202016.pdf.
23. Media reports, including "Chinese Media Playing the Victim of a 'Sinister Move' by the So-called Democracies, "Ganging up to Contain China's Rise", *South China Morning Post,* November 28, 2017, available at:
https://www.scmp.com/comment/insightopinion/article/2121907/indo-pacific-has-always-been-about-containing-rise-china.
24. "China Erases India Envoy's 'Renaming CPEC' Remark from Embassy Website, *Live Mint*, May 10, 2017, available at:
https://www.livemint.com/Politics/apU13YVBm03bHlmh0SnFaJ/China-erases-India-envoys-renaming-CPEC-remark-from-missi.html.
25. Various media reports, including "Quadrilateral Talks Involving India not about Containing China, says US", Zee News website, November 6, 2017, available at:
https://zeenews.india.com/asia/quadrilateral-talks-involving-india-not-about-containing-china-says-us-2054592.html.
26. "The 'Community of Common Destiny' in Xi Jinping's New Era" by Jacob Mardell, *The Diplomat*, October 25, 2017, available at:
https://thediplomat.com/2017/10/the-community-of-common-destiny-in-xi-jinpings-new-era.
27. Japanese MOFA website, available at:
https://www.mofa.go.jp/s_sa/sw/in/page3e_000969.html.
28. "Australia, Japan and India Trilateral.....", *The Economic Times*, July 12, 2018, available at:
https://economictimes.indiatimes.com/news/defence/australia-japan-and-india-trilateral-in-delhi-on-december-12/articleshow/61840323.cms.
29. "Donald Trump Demanding Allies Hosting US Troops Cover Full Cost of Deployment Plus Some Extra", *The Telegraph,* March 8, 2019, available at:

https://www.telegraph.co.uk/news/2019/03/08/donald-trump-demanding-allies-hosting-us-troops-cover-full-cost.
30. "Japan's Abe Set to Change Country's Pacifist Policy", by Toko Sekiguchi, *The Wall Street Journal*, available at: https://www.wsj.com/articles/japans-abe-set-to-make-change-in-countrys-pacifist-policy-1404129400.
31. "India Keeps Australia Out of the Malabar Exercise Again", by Asha Sundaramurthy, *The Diplomat,* May 8, 2018, available at: https://thediplomat.com/2018/05/india-keeps-australia-out-of-the-malabar-exercise-again.
32. "Australia Re-joining Quad Will Not Advance Regional Prosperity, Unity", by Li Yang, *Global Times,* November 15, 2017, available at:
http://www.globaltimes.cn/content/1075382.shtml.
33. "Japan, South Korea and China Planning Annual Trilateral Summit in December Despite Tensions", *Japan Times,* available at: https://www.japantimes.co.jp/news/2019/08/05/national/politics-diplomacy/japan-china-south-korea-planning-trilateral-summit-december/#.XUubPugzbIU.
34. "India Insists Regional Comprehensive Economic Partnership Only if China Lifts Curbs on IT", *The Economic Times,* August 3, 2019.
35. Media reports, including "ASEAN-focused China Fund Raising up to $3 Billion for Silk Road Projects", Money Control website, January 23, 2018, available at:
https://www.moneycontrol.com/news/world/asean-focused-china-fund-raising-up-to-3-billion-for-silk-road-projects-sources-2488969.html.
36. "India Is the Weakest Link in the Quad", by Derek Grossman, *Foreign Policy,* July 23, 2018, available at:
https://foreignpolicy.com/2018/07/23/india-is-the-weakest-link-in-the-quad.
37. "Asian Strategic Review, 2015: India as a Security Provider", S.D. Muni and Vivek Chadha (eds.), Pentagon Press: New Delhi.
38. Finds mention in several analyses, including "Will Quad Fly? The Answer is in Beijing", by Ravi Velloor, *The Straits Times*, November 17, 2017, available at:
https://www.straitstimes.com/opinion/will-quad-fly-the-answer-is-in-beijing.

4

Strategic Significance of Bay of Bengal and Andaman and Nicobar Islands in India's Act East Policy

Commodore R.S. Vasan IN (Retd.)

India seems more determined to Act East after adopting the 'Look East Policy' decades ago. The aggressive intent and behaviour of China has impacted both regional and global security dynamics. It is more evident since Xi announced the ambitious Brick and Road Initiative spanning continents both over land and through the sea routes. The Asian economies are particularly vulnerable to the designs of China which does not hesitate to gain inroads by investing heavily to obtain leverages for the future. With heavy dependence on the SLOCs for exports and imports that sustain China's growth and economy, China would like to protect its interests in the Indian Ocean.

The maritime neighbours to India's east therefore have been targeted for furthering China's economic, military, political and strategic clout. The smaller economies namely Bangladesh, Myanmar, Sri Lanka and also other Southeast Asian countries are lured by cheque book diplomacy which comes along with promise of heavy FDIs in infrastructure. But countries are learning slowly from the experience of Sri Lanka which got into a debt trap compelling it to sell off 70 percent equity to Chinese company to manage the port.

China has supported its economic investments with greater forays by PLA Naval units in the Bay of Bengal and the Indian Ocean. Even the nuclear submarines have become a regular sight in Indian waters raising concerns in the Indian leadership.

It is here that India has a geographical advantage with the location of A&N Islands close to the mouth of the choke point at Malacca Straits. China's Malacca dilemma as it is referred to be about the fear of being stopped by the Indian Navy or other coalition forces that could change the face of land or sea warfare. The Tri Services command which is being given full attention is an important strategic outpost for India that has the ability to use the geographic advantage.

It is exactly this advantage enjoyed by India that China would like to address by engaging the Bay of Bengal littorals. China also would like to ensure that it has connectivity through ports in Myanmar/Bangladesh to transport oil/gas to its borders to overcome the Malacca dilemma. It is doing the same thing also in the Arabian Sea by investing in Gwadar and CPEC which would reduce the dependence on Malacca Straits.

So it is clear that both India and China would be competing to obtain better leverages in the Bay of Bengal by playing to their respective advantages. This paper seeks to examine the developing great game in the Bay of Bengal. A&N Islands would be central to some of the discussions in terms of India's military and strategic counters to China's thrust into India's neighbourhood.

The Bay of Bengal (BoB) is the largest Bay which has been historically important in shaping the destiny of the countries in the Bay with events cantered around India. Recorded history from the past bears witness to the exploits of sea farers from Eastern Indian States who ventured eastwards and established close contacts with the kingdoms of Southeast Asian countries. Some of the kingdoms from Southern and Eastern India were able to wield influence and even rule some portions in the south eastern sea board of India.

The historical/cultural relations in east and Southeast Asian countries including during the Sri Vijaya Empire [1] enabled spread of religious and cultural influences through trade all the way up to China and Japan. The Kalingas, Cholas, Pallava's and other kingdoms were able to use the seas to spread their power and influence. Sri Vijaya Empire [2] which lasted till the 14th century as the name suggests was also under the influence of Hindu kingdoms from India.

When one moves forward to the colonial era, the fact that it was Kolkata [3] that was the launch pad for establishment of the British Empire through the East India Company is indicative of the importance of the Bay in shaping the colonial history of India.

Statistically, twenty five percent of the world's population is concentrated in eight countries bordering the Bay. Approximately, 200 million people live along the coast and depend on fisheries. Sixty one percent of fishers live below the poverty line. It will continue to shape the destiny of the region.

Geographic proximity is a great factor in Bay of Bengal that makes the littorals strive for collective progress and development. The events from the days of early civilization have had a profound impact in steering the responses of the countries both as a collective region and also as independent entities when countries based on religion or ethnicity started becoming independent.

Sumatra is just 90 NM from the Indian southern post, Coco Island is on lease to China and China is known to deploy its eves dropping units to monitor missile launches and movements in the Andaman Sea and in Bay of Bengal. Both China and Myanmar appear to deny [4] any military use for this Island.

The Straits of Singapore and Malacca Straits (SOMS) is a stone's throw away from A&N Islands giving such advantage to the tri services command the only one of its kind in India. It is not just a forward maritime post for India but also an important strategic asset that has the potential to change the game plan of China which has its eyes set on its westward expansion through the Maritime Silk Route and also through economic engagements of the littorals in the Bay of Bengal.

However, addressing the "China Dilemma" [5] of securing its energy and trade routes through the SOMS will continue to be a top priority for the Chinese leadership and the PLA.

Strategic Importance and Recent Developments in the Bay of Bengal

The present day location of Chandipur for missile launch tests, Sri Harikota Space Launch Station, Nuclear Reactors on the East Coast, Strategic Naval base in Visakhapatnam which houses the SSN/SSBN assets of India, offshore oil exploration for energy security and the increasing coastal traffic under Sagarrmala, define the strategic and maritime importance of the Bay of Bengal.

Some of the recent developments in the Bay of Bengal in India's neighbourhood are indicative of the shape of things to come.

Bangladesh: The induction of Ming Class [6] Submarines (Type 035) by Bangladesh Navy at a cost of US$ 203 million has brought the Chinese closer to the Indian shores. While Bangladesh presently has excellent relations with India, China has been able to make inroads into vital areas of defence support for Bangladesh by offering attractive options. India after the initial euphoria associated with the liberation of Bangladesh appears to have lost out to China due to the ability of China to invest heavily with an eye on future requirements.

For the first time, PM of India visited Bangladesh in 45 years [7] indicating how successive Governments ignored a vital neighbour in the Bay of Bengal. However, discussions on issues of naval cooperation, possibility of coordinated patrolling along International Maritime Boundary Line (IMBL), bilateral maritime exercise, collaboration in hydrography and joint surveillance of the exclusive economic zone bode well for both sides and there is a need to sustain the momentum. By and large, there is a greater synergy between the two countries [8] though it seems to happen only when the present government is in power in Bangladesh.

There were six agreements signed during PM's visit to Bangladesh in 2015. These pertained to coastal shipping, and Protocol Inland Waterways Transit and Trade (PIWTT). SoPs signed in November 2015 included use of Chittagong and Mongla Blue Economy and Economic Cooperation through JWG, agreement between the two coast guards for maritime security and crime prevention, and MoU between CSIR and Dhaka University for Oceanic Research.

Myanmar: A total of eleven MoUs were signed during Modi's visit [9] in 2017 with Myanmar including maritime cooperation and exchange of white shipping information. Hence, India appears to be acting East with greater sense of urgency than in the past.

Indonesia: Indonesia is another very important maritime neighbour with whom we have excellent cultural and historical relations, have not been harnessed fully. Indonesia is the largest trading partner of India in the Association of Southeast Asian Nations (ASEAN) regional bloc. Bilateral trade between the two countries increased from US$ 4.3 billion in 2005-06 to US$ 17 billion in 2016-17. Modi and Widodo [10] "discussed intensifying ties in trade and investment, defence and maritime cooperation". India has to intensify its efforts to build even stronger relations with Indonesia which is a fast growing economy and is an important partner in ASEAN.

Thailand: Cooperation with Thailand covers many areas, as discussed during the visit of Thai PM, including maritime security cooperation, joint defence production, counter-terrorism strategy and boosting trade and investment.

Chinese Interests

Chinese have shown great interest in developing ports in Bangladesh, Myanmar, Thailand, and Sri Lanka to get a foot hold and to serve long-term IOR ambitions. The MSR is being used as a conduit for fuelling the IOR ambitions of China.

Though the continued interest in Kra Isthamus is nothing new, the Chinese have not abandoned this dream project to overcome the Malacca dilemma.Greater deployment of PLA N units including nuclear submarines in the western Indian Ocean [11] has become a regular pattern and has raised concerns in the Indian establishment.

Rohingya crisis has affected Bangladesh, Myanmar and the destination countries for the refugees differently and will continue to be an issue of great interest for both India and China. While India is loooking at the demographic changes and security challenges within its borders, China is interested in ensuring that the crisis does not affect its interests in the port facility plans along the coast of Myanmar.

Search and Rescue (SAR)

The incident of MH 370, Air Asia plane and more recently the loss of a Coast Guard Dornier and AN 32 of the Indian Air Force in the Bay of Bengal clearly reinforces the belief that more needs to be done to strengthen the SAR architecture. Related to the MH 370 issue, Chinese analysts have linked this also to the Maritime Silk Route challenges as the ASEAN members [12] involved in the SAR operations post-MH 370 realised that there are greater challenges in coordination and preparation for such contingencies. Each nation in the region who are also members of the ICAO and also signatories of the M-SAR convention have a major responsibility in promoting the SAR architecture. This would mean using all resources including the military surveillance means to optimize the combined civil military efforts in peace time.

HADR

The need for having effective HADR architecture in the area that is prone to tsunamis, cyclones and flooding during monsoons is inescapable. The experience of Tsunami of 2004, cyclone Nargis and the cyclone which hit the city of Vizag on the east coast of India in 2014 are illustrative of the damage that can be caused by nature. It is evident that a lot of damage is accentuated due to manmade interventions. The Tsuami warning centre set up by India is working well and would provide the necessary warning to the countries in the region.

The data buoy programme of NIOT along with tsunami buoys [13] for providing timely warning has provided a 24x7 mechamism to warn the mainland and other countries in the event of a major earthquake in the Jawa Sumatra region which invariably can result in a tsunami depending on the level of the quake.

Challenges/Opportunities in the Bay of Bengal

With the unbridled expansion of China's interests from Asia to Africa, China has ambitious plans for connecting countries both through the sea routes and over the land. This has brought China to countries in the BoB with long-term investments and engagement. A major thrust is in developing ports in Bangladesh, Myanmar and Sri Lanka which in addition to facilitating movement of trade will also enable China to establish its foot print in the Indian Ocean.

The new Quadrilateral Initiative [14] which was abandoned after the initial euphoria in 2007 has come back, driven also by the enormous strides taken by China to cajol and engage with the smaller countries who are coming under the influence of China in a big way. This is seen as a big challenge by the members of the QUAD and therefore there is serious attempt to provide alternatives to the Belt and Road Initiative. However, the success of QUAD does not lie in the military hand shake but by other means which offer avenues for engaging with the smaller nations who are also looking at more benign investments in their countries to avoid heavy debt trap as experienced by Sri Lanka.

Illegal, Unregulated, Unmonitored (IUU) Fishing

With the dwindling stocks of fish in the region, there is greater conflict and competition amongst the fishers. The poaching in each other's territory causes tension and is a challenge for the security agencies. The regular issues in the

Palk Bay is indicative of the potential to derail bilateral relations due to the incursions into Sri Lankan territory by Indian fishermen. The issue of illegal unreported and unregulated (IUU) fishing has become a major issue for all nations in the region and requires coordinated efforts to promote responsible fishing on one hand and ensure that this activity is not misused for terrorist activities. The fishermen from the countries in the region routinely trespass into each other's territory complicating livelihood and security issues. The initiative between India and Pakistan to set up a hotline between the Coast Guard and the MSA of Pakistan has gone a long way in CBMs besides alleviating the sufferings of the fishing community on both the sides.

As opposed to detention and harassment, the erring fishermen are invariably escorted out of the respective territories through mutual consultation. However, the issue in the Palk bay is more complex as Tamil Nadu fishermen continue to cross the IMBL, claiming historical rights to the entire Palk bay though the IMBL was demarcated in 1974. The issue has always been a political one with the regional parties vying with each other to build constituencies and vote banks. It is not to say that there are no efforts to bring about an amicable solution. Fishermen on both the sides and NGOs have been in dialogue to work on the processes to resolve the decades old intransigence. Even Sri Lanka was indicted [15] for its practices of indulging in IUU.

Connectivity Isues

This has been the bane of the North-Eastern states of India which have serious limitations in movement of trade and people due to the geographic limitations. The infrastrcture continues to be woefullly inadequate and has affected the total integration of the region. The countries in the region are still resolving border control to effectively thwart people/cattle smuggling, illegal trade, drug and narcotics movement and terrorists using both land and sea routes for infiltration.

Challenges for the Countries in BIMSTEC

Coming to the BIMSTEC, Bhutan and Nepal are land locked and have completely different range of challenges both due to connectivity, terrain and neighbourhood. There are other domestic challenges in the backdrop of the geopolitical and geostrategic imperatives of the region.

The major challenges faced by the maritime nations of BIMSTEC in addition to the threat of seaborne attack, include many non-traditional threats like piracy, armed robbery, people smuggling, poaching, smuggling and marine pollution. These have engaged the attention of the policymakers with increased awareness of the potential of non-state actors to disrupt seaborne trade and commerce.

It would be in order to examine the statistics of last year in terms of the number of armed attacks and piracy in the world. As per the end of the year report for 2017 published by Regional Cooperation Agreement on Combating Armed Robbery and Piracy (ReCAAP) in Asia, the number of such attacks along the African coast has come down—it has gone up in the Bay of Bengal, South China Sea and Straits of Malacca. It is due to the increased number of such incidents in the past that ReCAAP was commissioned in Singapore. Officers from the regional navies and the coast guards are deputed both to the ReCAAP and the information fusion centre (IFC) to ensure that there is clear understanding of the local issues and the nations of the region work together to provide updates and analysis on the issues of piracy and armed robbery in Asia.

There has been a spate of attempts to use the sea routes for people smuggling. Many Sri Lankan Tamil Refugees have been lured to take this arduous journey in unseaworthy vessels through the sea routes using some of the member countries of BIMSTEC to reach Australia. Indian maritime agencies have been able to thwart such attempts by close coordination with the intelligence agencies. There are also issues of trafficking of women and children from Bangladesh and Nepal in to India.

There is a need to have a template for exchange of intelligence and information within the BIMSTEC structure and strengthen the process to ensure that innocents do not lose their lives due to this misadventure aided by fly by night operators.

The offer of the PM of India to provide a SAARC satellite surveillance system for promoting maritime safety needs to be considered on a priority basis and made available to the Bay of Bengal littorals.

The example of India which has been able to utilize its expertise in remote sensing in space has helped in facilitating processes for various purposes such as city planning, checking green cover, sea erosion, post natural calamity assessment etc. The system of telemedicine being offered in remote places in India by ISRO needs to be replicated in the remote areas of the BIMSTEC countries also through extensive network of nodes with the assistance of India which has demonstrated excellent skills in both space-based surveillance and adoptability to IT-enabled structures. Pakistan as a member of SAARC had reservations about such a system, but the countries in the Bay of Bengal should have no such concerns as it would be a transparent system with the active participation of the experts from the member countries who can derive the benefits of remote sensing.

Energy Security

If there is one commodity that will drive the economic progress and development of nations, it is the continued supply of energy products. India and China have become huge importers of oil, gas and coal. This is set to keep increasing exponentially as per the study of Energy Impact Analysis (EIA) year after year. The need for energy while challenging nations has also spurred research and development in scouting for both conventional and non-conventional energy sources. The discovery of the processes for extraction of shale oil and gas has liberated USA from the dependence on Middle East for energy products. The R&D on solar, wind, tide energy has been given a fillip with new advances in technology. However, the safe transportation of the energy goods and security will continue to be major factors of concern for all the nations.

Collectively, the countries in the region are in a position to invest in the related areas of research for exploring all avenues for meeting the energy demands of the nations in the region. The strength of each country can be leveraged to bring about optimal utilization of energy resources without serious impact on the environment. There is also a need to examine the inland water connectivity issues which can provide eco-friendly alternatives for transportation. There is a need to examine the practices in each country and evolve the best practices for promotion of the inland waterways.

Blue Economy

A lot has been said and written about the importance of blue economy in the century of the seas. The prosperity and development of nations is increasingly dependent on the oceans. The harnessing of the oceans for both living and non-living resources will see manifold increase as new technologies are applied in the maritime domain. The revolution in marine transportation, modernization of the related ports and infrastructure will redefine the parameters of maritime trade. It is necessary to integrate even land locked countries in this process. From this point of view, the specific and the most important recommendation for BIMSTEC is to provide opportunities for Bhutan and Nepal which are land locked to raise their merchant fleets manned by their citizens. This is allowed as per the United Nations Conventions on the Laws of the Sea. [16] India should take a lead and provide finances through a separate Blue Economy fund to be administered by BIMSTEC to facilitate this process of transformation of land locked countries as de facto maritime entities. Bangladesh or Sri Lanka could be the co-chair of this initiative which will have long-term impact on the objectives of BIMSTEC. Other member countries with capacity and capability in the maritime areas should open up their port facilities, training facilities and infrastructure for use by the land locked countries at concessional rates.

There are provisions in the United Nations Conventions on the Laws of the Seas (UNCLOS 1982) which allows for such provisions in respect of land locked countries. There is also a phenomenal increase in the commercial activity in the maritime domain, thanks to the initiatives such as the blue economy, and Chinese initiatives such as OBOR, MSR etc. There is a need to closely monitor the environmental impact of such initiatives as there could be compromises due to commercial interests of the stakeholders.

ASEAN as a block has great opportunities and potential to be tapped by India. ASEAN both as a group and also as individual countries of the group will continue to balance India-China power play. BoB countries will continue to play a pivotal role in India's 'Look East Policy' provided India is proactive and overcomes its reluctance to be a lead player in an area of both historical and contemporary importance to the future of the region. The participation of all the ASEAN heads [17] during the Republic Day celebrations in India has given a fillip to the India's 'Act East Policy'.

Andaman and Nicobar Islands

A&N Islands has provided India with an enviable geostrategic advantage in the BoB. After the British left India, it became part of India in 1950 and became a Union Territory of India in 1956. Recorded Indian history of these Islands brings out the role of Cholas and Marathas who owned these Islands and used them for furthering their strategic ambitions. Rajendra Chola (1014-1042 CE) conquered the A&N Islands [18] and used this to wage wars against the Sri Wijaya Empire in Sumatra. In the 17th century, this was used as a Maratha base by the Maratha Admiral Kanhoji Angre who fought valiantly against the British and the Dutch. The Navy has named a base on the west coast of India in the honour of this Maratha Admiral who ruled the seas. He is even credited with annexing these Islands to India.

China is concerned with its vulnerability through the Malacca Straits into the Indian Ocean since it passes under the watchful eyes of the Tri Services command in Port Blair. The Tri services Command is watching the movement of all of China's merchant and war ships as they are on passage through the Sea Lines of Communication.(SLOCs). Concerned with SLOC safety and energy security, China is closely monitoring the developments in A&N Islands. It even considers this geographic advantage of India as a thorn to its Indian Ocean ambitions.

The importance of the A&N Islands cannot be overstated in the ever changing maritime dynamics in the South China Sea and also the Indian Ocean. While the Pacific and the Indian Ocean are connected through the Malacca Straits, India has its Tri Services command—the only joint command in Port Blair. On the face of it, it is evident that India enjoys a geographic advantage in the Indian Ocean due to the possession of Island both in the Bay of Bengal and also in the Arabian Sea. While a lot has been done to ensure that these Islands are well protected and provide India with the advance warning and response capability, there is a need to shore up the Command, Control, Communication, Computer, Intelligence, Inter-operability, Surveillance and Reconnaissance (C4I2SR) architecture in the area to ensure that there are no surprises by the Chinese who already have a token presence in the Coco Islands on lease from Myanmar in the Andaman Sea. In this context, the importance of setting up a Radar Station in Narcondam Island has been covered by this author in an analysis carried both by SAAG and C3S.

With the heavy sea traffic through the 10 degree channel and the Andaman Sea, the fragile marine environment around the A&N Islands also needs to be protected and there is a need for coordinated action led by the Tri Services Command by involving the nearby Southeast Asian countries. It has been suggested that there is an immediate need to initiate coordinated and cooperative measures through the biennial useful maritime forum Milan in Port Blair. [19] The post-tsunami assistance for affected nations and the initiative in setting up of the tsunami warning facility by India has been well received by the countries of the region. Also there is scope for sub-regional Search and Rescue (SAR) mechanism to be put in place by involving the countries of the region post the disappearance of MH 370 which exposed chinks in the SAR architecture.

Strategic Significance

The group of islands known as Andaman and Nicobar Islands are of great strategic importance to India due to its close proximity to the Malacca Straits, the gateway to international trade and commerce through the waterways in Southeast Asia. The group of Islands is administered by the Lt. Governor and is considered as a union territory. As far as the military presence is concerned, it is now administered by the Tri Services command which was set up in 2001. The area was previously governed by the Navy and the senior most officer of the rank of Vice Admiral was designated as the Fortress Commander, A&N Islands. The command of the A&N now is on rotational basis, managed by the three services. The Tri Services command has all the three services and also the Indian Coast Guard which is charged with duties related to the maritime zones of India. The Coast Guard has many stations/posts around the Island chain to ensure that it is able to discharge its duties as provided in the Maritime Zones of India Act of 1976.

The dependence on the choke points is of critical importance to all the nations of the world. Any disruption of traffic through the choke points would affect economy and trade. The volume of Chinese goods moving in and out of Malacca Straits is the highest in the region and China cannot ill-afford to have any disruptions affecting its trade and transit. According to the present estimates, there are over 60,000 ships

[20] that use the Malacca Straits annually both ways carrying critical energy products and also other items of trade and commerce. Andaman and Nicobar group therefore provides the geographic advantage of being an outpost close to Malacca Straits and other straits in Southeast Asia to provide any advance information/warning about impending movements through the choke points.

Chinese Concerns

From the Chinese point of view, it views with concern any developments in the A&N region. Geography confers great advantage in the Indian Ocean Region to India as it is in a position to monitor all the activities not only from the mainland but also from the outposts in West and East. So Andaman and Nicobar Islands provide that ability to monitor the movement of all vessels to and from the Indian Ocean through the Malacca Straits or any other choke point in the region. While it has the capability to interdict any traffic, even India believes in a peaceful periphery and would not indulge in any disruption unless there is a spill over of the land battle to the seas. It is, therefore, in the interest of both the nations to work together and resolve the border dispute at an early date in a time bound manner.

India's Concerns about Chinese Presence

For decades, there has been mutual suspicion on the presence of Chinese monitoring agencies in Coco Islands which was leased by Myanmar to China. Coco Islands has a runway and for long, this small island has been the hub of listening activity by the Chinese. The missile and space experiments on the east coast are also susceptible to monitoring by appropriate equipment that can be airlifted to the Island as required and ships that could be deployed around Coco Islands. Myanmar enjoys good relations with China and is the beneficiary of increased assistance and cooperation particularly when the West shunned Myanmar in the past due to the military rule and what it considered as a stumbling block to establishment of democracy.

China has also shown increased interest in the recent decades to engage with India's maritime neighbours. Some of the western analysts have gone to the extent of terming this as the 'string of pearls' strategy or even a noose around India. The author of this paper does not endorse the concept of 'string of pearls' or the intentions ascribed to the engagement of Chinese presence in the Indian Ocean. China and India are both huge importers of energy products through the sea routes. With increased dependence on the sea routes for trade and transit, China has initiated certain measures to secure sea lines and the choke points.

Evidently, the economic investments in Hambanthota, Gwadar, Bangladesh, Myanmar and Maldives are both to enhance the value of economic engagement with the Asian smaller neighbours and use the economic leverage so acquired for strategic advantage as and when required in the future. Purely translated, this would mean that at a future date, PLA Navy units would have the option of staging through the deep water ports in the region where these have been built with Chinese assistance and financial help to serve Chinese national interests. It is this possibility that is being factored in the strategic calculus of Indian Ocean dynamics.

Way Ahead: BoB Initiatives

There is a need to proactively increase connectivity through North-East including inland waterways which has great potential to bring about greater integration and connectivity to promote trade and linkages.

India will need to work with other developing economies in the region for proactive engagement of littorals in BoB for collective growth and prosperity. Providing greater avenues for the BoB states to utilize the soft and hard power capability of India for furthering their own standing will contribute to the collective growth of the region and will also establish India's pre-eminence in the region.

From the point of view of HADR and SAR enhancing capacity, capability and effectiveness of response mechanisms would overcome some of the limitations of the region in handling emergencies, contingencies and disasters. India has the technical competence and capability to equip smaller nations with better monitoring and scouting architecture to enhance the maritime domain awareness.

Making the QUAD work is indeed challenging but will have greater chances of success if it is played at the strategic, economic, political and military level in an inclusive manner without limiting the QUAD to just a military alliance of sorts.

In addition to enhancing scope of military and civil training to the neighbours, increased allocation for student and academic exchanges programmes with BoB countries would go a long way in nurturing people to people relations.

The most important of the BoB initiatives is related to ensuring that the forward post and launching pad namely the A&N Islands are equipped with the wherewithal to thwart any Chinese aggression and intent. BoB countries and the A&N Islands will play a pivotal role in complementing India's 'Act East Policy'.

Notes and References

1. "Southeast Asia: A Historical Encyclopaedia: From Angkor Wat to East", Volume 1, ABC Cleo: Denver, 2004, p. 11.
2. S.K. Lim (2001), "Asia Civilizations: Ancient to 1800 AD", Asiapac Books: Singapore, p. 148.
3. "Student's Britannica: India", Britannica India: New Delhi, 2000, p. 410.
4. Michael J. Strauss (2015), "Territorial Leasing in Diplomacy and International Law", Brill NIJHOF Leidon: Boston, p. 125.
5. Geoffrey Till, Emrys Chew and Joshua Ho (2009), "Globalization and Defence in the Asia-Pacific: Arms Across Asia", Routledge: London and New York, p. 81.
6. *The Diplomat*, available at:

https://thediplomat.com/2017/01/why-chinas-submarine-deal-with-bangladesh-matters.

7. *The Hindu*, available at: http://www.thehindu.com/todays-paper/tp-national/India-to-firm-up-defence-ties-with-Bangladesh/article16733501.ece.
8. Harsh V. Pant (2012), "The Rise of the Indian Navy: Internal Vulnerabilities, External Challenges", Routledge: London and New York, p. 116.
9. "There Appears to be a New Momentum to Engage with Myanmar", *The Hindustan Times*, c https://www.hindustantimes.com/india-news/five-reasons-why-narendra-modi-s-visit-to-myanmar-is-important/story-nRB2ljRqwvdcMcUtkdeHsK.html.
10. "Many Agreements Were Signed during Wododo's Visit to India and the Focus on Defence, Trade and Other Areas are Indicative of the Interest on Both Sides to Improve the Relations", available at: https://www.oneindia.com/india/india-indonesia-sign-agreements-on-strengthening-defence-economic-ties-2288632.html.
11. Roger Cliff (2015), "China's Military Power: Assessing Current and Future Capabilities", Cambridge University Press, p. 131.
12. Zhang, Jie (2017), "China's Belt and Road Initiatives and Its Neighbouring Diplomacy", World Scientific Publishing Company Private Limited: Singapore, p. 259.
13. "Annual Report of Earth Sciences", Government of India, 2008, p. 160.
14. Vijay Sakhuja and Kapil Narula (2016), "Maritime Dynamics in the Indo-Pacific", Vij Books India Limited: New Delhi, p. 73.
15. Patrick Peebles (2015), "Historical Dictionary of Sri Lanka", Rowman and Littlefield: Plymouth, p. 146.
16. Helmut Tuerk (2012), "Reflections on the Contemporary Law of the Sea", Martrinus NIJHOFF Publishers: Leidon-Boston, p. 53.
17. "The Analysis of Why ASEAN Heads Are Coming to India", *The Diplomat*, available at: https://thediplomat.com/2018/01/why-it-matters-that-asean-leaders-are-heading-to-india.
18. Matnur Lakshman Prasad (1968), "History of the Andaman and Nicobar Islands: 1756-1966", Sterling Publishers, p. 10.

19. Harsh V. Pant (2012), "The Rise of the Indian Navy: Internal Vulnerabilities, External Challenges", Routledge: London and New York, p. 45.
20. Wayne Talley (2008), "Maritime Safety, Security and Piracy", Informa: London, p. 91.

5

Indian Ocean Region and India's Act East Policy: Maritime Challenges for India in the 21st Century

Aswani R.S. and Mihir Das

This paper analyses the maritime dimensions of India's 'Act East Policy'. After the culmination of Cold War, the structural adjustments of 1990s coupled with the vacuum in the Indian Ocean Region attracted both regional and extra regional powers there. India always considered Indian Ocean as its backyard and China's revival of its ancient maritime Silk Route and Belt and Road Initiative has posed serious threats to India's big power ambitions. India views the extensive cultural and commercial relations that China builds with Indian Ocean littorals, as its strategically expansive efforts in the region. As a corollary, it could induce both political and security threats for India.

Hence, to match the Chinese policy of expansion, India needs a launch pad to improve its association with the Southeast Asian countries and certainly, the 'Act East Policy' offers one. This necessitates India to revamp its geostrategic goals for the 21st Century through an effective maritime policy that can strengthen India's security in its own backyard and integrate its aspirations into the wider spectrum of development, linking East Asia with South Asia. The remodelling of two decades old 'Look East Policy' into a more proactive policy is a good beginning for India to invigorate its role as a big power in the region and evolve as a benign friend of ASEAN and other Eastern nations. India ought to vigorously pursue extensive economic and defence cooperation with the Southeast to counter China and ensure a strong and stable presence in the Indian Ocean Region.

Introduction

The international order is always volatile, uncertain, complex and anomalous and thus it undergoes phases of equilibrium and disequilibrium. From a Euro centric global order, the centre of geopolitical power shifted to Asia in the 21st century, with the rise of giants like China and India. In recent times, in addition to nation states, major regional organizations have also become key strategic players. European Union unites European nations politically and economically to secure the continent for lasting peace. The 10-member Association of Southeast Asian Nations, better distinguished by its acronym ASEAN, is one such regional grouping that has become a powder keg for world politics. With tens of thousands of non-resident Indians living in these countries and over 50 percent of our foreign trade now directed here, East of Asia is of strategic significance for India's foreign policy and economic interests. In the post-Cold War era, owing to the transformation of India into a developed and prosperous country, India adopted the policy of Look East towards enhancing capacity building and facilitating greater cultural and people-to-people exchanges (Business Standard, 2015).

The 'Look East Policy' (LEP) stressed on regional integration, reforms and liberalization, rapid economic growth and development of the North-Eastern region of India, with focus on geographic nearness of countries, sub-regional collaboration and emphasis on free trade agreements (Bhattacharjee, 2016). The LEP has brought India proximate to the ASEAN nations; however, it was not completely capable and competent to knock the prospects that such associations could have provided.

On November 2014, India renamed its foreign policy with the Southeast Asian countries. While some scholars view this as old wine in a new bottle, a few others view it as a proactive step. An analysis of the trends of bilateral summits and economic exchanges show that 'Act East Policy' is a conscious upgradation of India's two-decade-old 'Look East Policy'. In the words of former Ambassador M. Ganapathi (2015), 'Look East is a passive adumbration; Act East incorporates greater action and dynamism'. 'Act East Policy' is considered a cornerstone in India's external relations. ASEAN and the far eastern countries are significant to India on multiple fronts. ASEAN is India's fourth largest trading partner, with ASEAN-India annual trade standing at over US$ 76 billion in 2013, having registered an average growth of 22 percent per annum over the last decade (Ram, 2013). In its current dimensions, the ASEAN-India Partnership encompasses three pillars: political-security, economic and socio-cultural (Roberts, Habir and Sebastian, 2015). India shares land border with an ASEAN member state, Myanmar and maritime boundaries with two other ASEAN member states viz., Indonesia and Thailand.

The economic and political growth of China as a big power in Asia, and as a super power, with potential to even challenge the position of United States has raised concerns in India. The timely revival of ancient maritime Silk Route and Belt and Road Initiative (BRI) has added to the apprehensions in India, which finds that a rising China profoundly challenges its position. The geostrategic landscape of world in general and Indian Ocean in particular, is changing rapidly. The mounting commercial and strategic relations that China is fostering in the Indian Ocean has raised alarms in New Delhi. Thus, while Indian Ocean has become a hotbed for global politics with increasing Chinese presence in the Indian Ocean Region (IOR) littorals, relations with Chinese neighbourhood becomes a matter of urgency for India to counter power China.

Hence, though 'Look East Policy' began with economic objectives, the transition to 'Act East' emphasises India's strategic objectives too. Policy makers and strategic analysts in Southeast Asia also point out the prerequisite to balance

China's swift growth by expediting a robust engagement with India. It is projected that the energy requirements of the world will rise by fifty percent through the end of this decade, with leading consumers being China and India. Indian Ocean offers its waters to transit the shipments and both India and China are building their maritime capital to ensure an unhindered movement of their goods and services.

The strategists on maritime security are seized with the military dimension of China's port construction across the Indian Ocean littorals to promote its Blue Economy. The IOR extends from the Red Sea to the Eastern side of the Pacific Ocean, and is famous for major choke points such as the Straits of Malacca and Strait of Hormuz. Though thickly populated, it is closer to the international shipping lanes and contributes extensively to major trade routes of the world. Experts feel that a stable, peaceful and tension-free IOR could be established through appropriate policy interventions that accommodate collective international shipping concerns to sail through IOR without a 'fear of interference' by any regional or extra-regional political actors. Furthermore, as per the United Nations guidelines, the seabed and its cherished resources are common possessions to be equitably accessed by all the littoral nations of IOR.

The United Nations Convention on the Law of the Sea (1982) includes guidelines on the autonomy of the high seas and the "common heritage of mankind" on the oceans. However, this reference to 'legitimate presence' is superfluous. It can thus, easily be understood that the dynamics of world commerce is changing, in alignment with the eastbound energy trade, with China and India being leading importers of oil in Asia (Kreft, 2006). This will have direct impact on the commercial accomplishments of IOR, as the Sea Lines of Communication (SLOCs) are vital for the trade of energy and growth of littorals in the IOR.

By the year 2025, China is anticipated to become major economy of the world, surpassing even the United States, provided the growth rates of China and India continue to be around 7-10 percent (Sweijs, et al., 2010). More than 50 percent of world's container movement and 70 percent of energy requirements are transported through IOR and it offers much cherished SLOCs between far East and far West countries (Madhavan, 2015). The world's leading three economies are situated in the Asian continent, viz. China, Japan and India with their critical trade originating from Central Asia.

In spite of possessing an extensive coastline and two archipelagos on both sides of the peninsula, India is accused historically, for being a 'sea blind nation' (Kumar, 2014). These features are strategic in the geopolitical scenario of the world and regardless of considering Indian Ocean as its backyard and India as the rightful authority of this maritime space; India has hardly undertaken a successful maritime policy. 'Whoever controls Indian Ocean will dominate the world' is a famous saying attributed to great American maritime strategist Alfred Mahan (Sempa, 2014).

Echoing the Mahanian visions, India's first maritime strategist K.M. Panikkar has also written on the significance of Indian Ocean in India's forward marching as a big power. Blue Economy is the word that is doing rounds amongst the strategists. Gunter Pauli, initiator of the term Blue Economy, states that it is a business model in the nature of an integrated matrix of amalgamation of social inclusion and environment sustainability, which symbolizes substantial reserves in costs and capital, despite eroding the 'ecological footprint' on the environment and bio-diversity loss, along with health risks to current and future generations (Pauli, 2010). Blue Economy is a globally prized concept that has appealed to the littorals of Indian Ocean Region and has ensured a healthy ocean providing higher productivity. India's 'Look East/Act East Policy', (Muni, 2012) which was of modest beginning in the early 1990s, devises its heritage in the profound and enduring historic and civilizational association amidst the countries of Southeast Asia and India.

The recorded manuscripts confirms that Indian Ocean opened its trade routes since 3 millennium BC and Indian culture and civilization spread around the world through these sea lanes. India was always the land of riches, which mesmerized merchants across the globe who flocked to the East in search of spices, gold and textiles. Sengupta (2017) has stated that for the seafaring traders for Indian origin, those far way islands (currently Southeast Asia) were highly striking for the umpteen treasures it held. The similarity between the tropical terrains of India and Southeast, led to many similarities in cultivation patterns. The presence of huge cardamom plantations and coconut cultivation led to Indian mercantile class naming them *Narikeldeep* and *Tokola*.

The mythical presence of gold even led them to call it as *Swarnabhumi*. The folklores of Odisha sing many a fable about lands east of the Ocean. The annual Bali Jatra (Voyage to Bali) is a festival conducted in Odisha, on the *Kartik Purnima* day (Mohapatra, 2007) to take advantage of the wind blowing during this time in the Bay of Bengal. Bali, a small island in Indonesia has a majority of Hindu population, whereas Indonesia is well celebrated as the world's largest Muslim populated country. The popular reign of Kalinga dynasty and Chola dynasty has records of spreading their influence across the Indian Ocean to the Southeast Asian nations. The Prambanam temple, Borobudur temple, Pagan temple and the most popular Angkor Wat temple indicates the historical and in-depth connection these provinces cherished, not merely in political, but also in the realms of art and architecture too (Sengupta, 2017).

In addition to the cultural exchanges, Indian ports along the Coromandel Coast had trading relations with East and Southeast Asian ports since centuries. However, the advent of Europeans in the South of Asia caused a degeneration of hitherto existing regional exchanges between these rulers.

Colonial powers from the west took over India's maritime trade and vocation by force. The British colonial rule in India reduced the Indian Ocean to a British Lake and the country under colonial-rule had to turn westward. Post-Independence, India had to deal with multitudes of internal problems and it always looked west for economic, technological and political support. During the period of Cold War, even though India formulated and propagated the non-alignment policy, it positioned closer to Soviet Union for technological assistance whereas Southeast Asia geared closer to US, which made no close relations possible between these parties.

Post-Cold War Changes in Southeast Asia

The economies of Southeast Asia have acquired ample purchasing power in the previous decades and this has engaged them in an era of economic boom, which led to a need for securing their energy-supply lines. Putten, Wetzling, Kamerling (2014), opine that such tendencies affect the major SLOCs of Southeast Asia that run through the Indian Ocean such as the Strait of Bab-el-Mandeb, Malacca and Hormuz. The political and commercial competition in the region has led to an increasing presence of naval vessels in the region for patrolling and monitoring activities.

This practice encompasses regional co-operations such as European Union, but not limited to, United States, Russia, China, India, Australia and Japan. These above mentioned powers are gradually ensuring their military existence in the region for major strategic goals that are not only commercial in nature, but also political. The rim of the Indian Ocean thus is under the radar of these nations for their geopolitical manifestation (Malik and Nunes, 2016). This region is strategically significant for many smaller navies such as Singapore, Malaysia and Pakistan also, and they are steadily aiming at increasing their presence in the region. The presence of a 'security dilemma' is acute in the IOR, as mutual distrust and geopolitical competitions, harbour suspicions that could turn highly problematic. The IMO had been publicizing the 'safer seas and cleaner oceans' for many decades. But the absence of cooperation amidst the regional powers and the lack of effective multilateral agreements on 'safer seas and human security' apparently was a major deterrent to establish a peaceful IOR (Putten, 2014).

The ocean around India had been the cauldron of political activities involving mega powers and also there had been physical intrusions in nearly unmarked regions in the sea. Thus, the tensions have become acute and apparently the zone is considered perilous with the presence of conventional and nuclear vessels that had been used by major powers in showcasing their strategic positioning and staging a permanent presence in the area. Naval task forces, because of their inherent mobility, were able to constitute a powerful projection of military might. Many of the nations in this region are averse to 'Gunboat Diplomacy and Domination' by military forces, which they faced some time before. This is certainly reasonable and rational. As the region is an established sea lane for cargo and all kinds of vessels for the East-West route; competition and rivalry have become new trends in international politics across this IOR. These thoughts were planted possibly by the colonial powers when they needed to dislodge the existing power from enjoying the fruits of colonization.

For champions of peace throughout the world, demilitarization of the Indian Ocean (Sakhuja, 2014) would mean elimination of one of the world's most dangerous hot beds of tension. This however did not happen. The safeguarding of vital interest of the big powers provided to them enough justification for an unprecedented escalation of military presence in the area. There was a time when the vacuum theory (O'Loughlin, 2000) was universally peddled by the western powers and their mass media. It postulated that the withdrawal of British naval power from the Indian Ocean would create a void if not filled by the United States and its allies and would invite Soviet presence. The 'vacuum theory' is seldom mentioned now, but somewhere the ghost still remains around.

Chinese Expansionism in the Indian Ocean

The Asia-Pacific is today one of the fastest growing regions of the world, showing unparalleled dynamism in political, security, economic and demographic terms. It has truly emerged as the economic and geopolitical centre of gravity for the world in the 21st century. Some of the dominant trends shaping this reality include the rise of a number of new powers in Asia, notably China, the re-balancing or "pivot to Asia" strategy of the United States, and a regional economic and strategic architecture seeking to define itself with strong currents of multilateralism. China had opened her economy in 1978 and achieved nearly 10 percent economic growth for three decades. This had allowed an impeccable globalization of her economy (Wearden, 2010). China has lifted 300 million people out of poverty and has consequently emerged as the second largest economy of the world after the United States; and Japan being pushed to the third position. With the advancement in economic growth, China's global influence is also on the rise.

As for now, China's principal interest seems to lie in the need for protecting the SLOCs along the Indian Ocean and to maintain uninterrupted supply of trade and energy resources. In fact, China surpassed the US in 2013 to become the world's largest oil importing country (Johnson, 2015). To ensure the security of the choke points of Indian Ocean, mainly Malacca Strait and Lombok Strait in the East and Bab El-Mandab in the West, the design of the Maritime Silk Route is being propagated. As a part of her strategic assessment of the region, China has been considering that both India and the United States are better placed in the Indian Ocean Region because of different reasons and in order to bolster her presence in the Indian Ocean Region, China has initiated a policy of seeking level facilities and strategic partnership with the littoral states surrounding India. Xi Jinping, in his first policy speech as Chairman of the Communist Party of China, stated in January 2013 that, "No foreign country should ever nurse hopes that we will bargain over our core national interests" (Buckley, 2013).

Since China has maritime disputes with all its neighbours in the Pacific Ocean, the strategic maritime collaboration is being cultivated in with the littoral states of the Indian Ocean. Under the strategy, China has availed naval facilities at Gwadar Port in Pakistan, electronic gathering facilities on islands in the Bay of Bengal, port facilities in Hambantota in Sri Lanka and Chittagong in Bangladesh, naval bases in Myanmar, funding of the construction of canal and signing of the military agreement with Cambodia and so on. Pakistan is a strategic ally and always a friend of China who is building road and rail link from Gwadar Port to Mainland China through Pakistan Occupied Kashmir (POK)—an area also claimed by India (Jain, 2017).

In addition to port buildings, China's naval modernization efforts is also a matter of concern for India as it is a broad-based effort that includes a wide array of platform and weapon acquisition programs, including programs for ASBMs, anti-ship cruise missiles (ASCMs), land-attack cruise missiles (LACMs), surface-to-air missiles, mines, manned aircrafts, submarines, aircraft carriers, destroyers, frigates, corvettes, patrol crafts, amphibious ships, mine countermeasures (MCM) ships, underway replenishment ships, hospital ships, unmanned vehicles (UVs), and supporting C4ISR9 systems (O'Rourke, 2017).

Since its Independence in 1949 until the mid-1980s, China's naval operations were limited to coastal defence. By the end of 1980s, China sought to expand its naval capabilities beyond the coastal waters. The PLAN in 2016 conducted its first naval exercises with Cambodia and it now conducts routine surface deployments in the South China and Philippine Seas—including an unprecedented seven deployments in the

Philippine Sea in 2012 and nine deployments in 2013. Far seas training and deployments has become the new norm for China's navy.

As the Department of Defence, in USA states, 'Over the next decade, China may construct a new Type 095 nuclear powered, guided-missile attack submarine (SSBN), which not only would improve the PLA Navy's anti-surface warfare capability, but might also provide it with a more clandestine, land-attack option' (Business Insider, June 17, 2016). China's DF-21D "Carrier Killer" ballistic missile has a range of about 810 nautical miles and the force has acquired 12 of Russia's Kilo-class diesel-electric submarines for its conventional weaponry. China has also launched two diesel-electric (Song and Yuan class), and two nuclear classes (Jin and Shang class) submarines.

The growth of PLAN has been slow and steady and has become the largest navy in Asia, today with more than 300 surface ships, submarines, amphibious ships, and patrol crafts. Though China had only one ballistic missile submarine in 2008, the figure had grown up to four in 8 years. Until 2014, China had no corvettes (i.e., light frigates), but by November 2017, the figures has gone up at a rapid rate to 37. By 2015, the PLAN submarine force consisted of five nuclear attack submarines, four nuclear ballistic missile submarines, and 57 diesel attack submarines (ONI Report, 2015).

To effectively employ sophisticated naval platforms and long-range weaponry, any modern navy requires an advanced maritime command, control, computers, communication, intelligence, surveillance, and reconnaissance (C4ISR) capability (O'Rourke, 2017). China's interest in Indian Ocean periphery can be understood in this context. China's ambitious naval modernization during the past 15 years, added with the porous borders of India, naturally raise alarms in New Delhi.

This spectacular rise of China over the past two decades has changed the geopolitical scene across India's maritime frontiers. It is true that China has a legitimate interest in ensuring the security of its frontiers. Nevertheless, what has disturbed the entire maritime neighbourhood of Southeast Asia has been Beijing's readiness to deploy its navy coercively to enforce its expansionist claims across the South China Sea. These claims, spelt out in a unilaterally drawn "Nine Dotted Line" (Tsirbas, 2016) has resulted in tensions with virtually all the neighbours, including South Korea, Japan, Taiwan, the Philippines, Vietnam, Brunei, Malaysia and Indonesia.

It also seems to be a part of a very "aggressive strategy" that China is even building air bases and artificially constructed islands across the South China Sea to enforce its untenable claims (Rolf and Agnew, 2016). This claim has been rejected by a UN tribunal in a judgment on a complaint filed by the Philippines. Japan, Vietnam and Indonesia alone have stood firm against Chinese expansionism. Indonesia could well take China to an international tribunal over Beijing's claims to its Natuna Islands and these conflicts assert the fact that the overarching imagery China draws out for itself lacks a concrete ground, at least in its neighbourhood.

Undue Publicity of the Maritime Silk Route

The vigorous propaganda attached to the Maritime Silk Route of China highlights that China is keen to show its "assertiveness" on its maritime boundary claims across the South China Sea and this is accompanied by its growing naval presence, including nuclear submarines, across the sea-lanes of the Indian Ocean, extending till the Straits of Aden. Incidentally, China has established a naval base in Djibouti, across the Straits of Hormuz, to the Straits of Malacca. SLOCs in the entire Indian Ocean Region extending from Aden to Malacca account for 40 percent of the world's oil production and 57 percent of the world's oil trade (Khalid, 2012). Seventy percent of India's oil supplies comes through these sea-lanes and around 7 million Indians reside in the Gulf countries, from where India receives over US$ 40 billion annually, as remittances (Parthasarathy, 2017b).

It is true that India had been maintaining stability of its maritime frontiers as extending across the Indian Ocean, from Aden to Malacca Straits. With the recent rise of Chinese power and territorial assertiveness, the situation has become a matter of concern and worry for India. These interventions and the apparent likelihood of expansionism can only be tackled politically but backed by a solid military strategy. There was a time when one of the Chinese Admirals claimed that, "The Indian Ocean is not India's Ocean" (Yi, 2015).

This was when concern was expressed by India over China using its clout with Myanmar to establish bases and monitoring facilities in the Cocos Islands near the Andaman and Nicobar Islands and possibly in Myanmar's Bay of Bengal port of Kyaukpyu. The construction of Kaladan corridor as a part of the 'Act East Policy' (Pattnaik, 2017) is meant to be a deterrent to such similar advances. While India has never claimed that the Indian Ocean is "India's Ocean", China has claimed that bulk of the South China Sea is "China's Sea" and even extended its claim to Indonesia's shores. Combined with these claims, the full-fledged military base in Djibouti, and full access to port facilities at Gwadar, in Baluchistan, China is set to significantly strengthen Pakistan's navy, providing it with 4 frigates and 8 submarines.

India's Collaborations in Indian Ocean

It is a matter of pride that India is admired globally for settling its maritime boundaries with all its neighbours including Bangladesh, Myanmar, Thailand, Malaysia, Indonesia, Sri Lanka and Maldives. Moreover, India has no maritime boundary tensions with Pakistan, though the maritime boundary can be demarcated only after the land boundary is agreed upon. During the last decade, Indian Navy has many success stories of going an extra mile in the littoral states to support them in times of cyclones, tsunami or similar disasters. If India wants to establish itself as a benign power in

Asia, it will be very important to continue with these moves so that the bitterness does not set in.

Additionally, the Indian Navy also has been giving support in terms of training and exercises to make these States largely independent and enabling them for future strategic moves. It is obvious, however, that the Indian Ocean's security environment is heating up. China's across-the-board investments in expeditionary maritime power-projection capabilities (including infrastructure) and in sea-denial capabilities serve a variety of peaceful as well as potentially confrontational purposes. Along with China, India is correspondingly investing heavily in nuclear-attack submarines. In terms of military capabilities, these submarines ought not to be a choice since the end of the Cold War. Thus, it is fair to say that this indicates a return to great-power politics in a more traditional sense.

In 2017, a naval conclave was held in Goa from October 31 to November 2 which was attended by senior naval officials of Myanmar, Indonesia, Malaysia, Singapore, Bangladesh, Thailand, Sri Lanka, Mauritius, Seychelles, and Maldives. In the conclave, India had promised access to better exchange of information, including timely intelligence on maritime movements across the Indian Ocean. It was also decided in the conclave that analogous steps should be taken for cooperation with oil-producing/energy partners of India (Defence Minister Speaks, 2017).

In May 2017, navies of India and Singapore undertook a seven day long mega maritime exercise in the South China Sea especially because this area had been seeing an enhanced Chinese presence; oftentimes fraught with some amount of aggressiveness. Four warships of the Indian Navy and long range anti-submarine warfare aircraft P-8l participated in the SIMBEX (Singapore-India Maritime Bilateral Exercise), and this was a step towards achieving closer coordination between these two navies and could reach a state when inter-operability could also be thought of. Such exercises are being held since 1994 and it was the 24th edition of the annual exercise between the two countries (SIMBEX 2017 concludes, 2017). The Chinese are extremely averse to any passage of US naval ships that passes through this area, even though the state maintains that there is no threat to "freedom of navigation".

Thus, it is imperative that in spite of India professing for non-alignment—the country had been acting on strategic dimensions of security in maritime. While trilateral naval exercises with the US and Japan are now undertaken regularly and maritime cooperation with the US is set to continue, it remains to be seen how Australia can be integrated into this group.

India and Russia in 2017, successfully conducted iteration of the joint Indra military drill held from October 19 to 29 near Vladivostok in Russia, the Indian Ministry of Defence said in a November 1 statement. The bilateral military drill, which took place at training sites near Vladivostok and in the Sea of Japan, involved over 900 Indian military personnel from the Indian Army, Air Force, and Navy, two IL 76 aircraft, as well as two surface warships. Russia dispatched over 1,000 troops from all three services including warships from the Pacific Fleet and aircraft from Russia's Eastern Military District (Ministry of Defence [MoD], 2017). With around 40 percent of India's exports proceeding beyond Malacca through the Asia-Pacific Region, it is only appropriate that it has an appropriate architecture for security/military cooperation in place on the eastern shores of Asia, across what is now called the Indo-Pacific Region.

China's much-publicized OBOR initiative possibly could enable Beijing to dominate the SLOCs of the Western Pacific and Indian Oceans by extending credits which the recipients cannot repay. Huge investment was granted to Sri Lanka in the port at Hambantota (Smith, 2016). This decision has been internally criticized in Colombo but other recipients of Chinese 'aid' will find themselves caught in a 'debt trap' wherein they are increasingly forced to compromise their sovereignty and hand over control of infrastructure and industries to the

Chinese. Some of the Pakistani economists are now questioning the economic wisdom of receiving Chinese 'assistance' of over US$ $46 billion, largely at near commercial terms (Kohli, 2016). Similar concerns have been voiced in Myanmar. Unfortunately, in Pakistan, such major decisions on Chinese cooperation are taken by the army top brass, who may not be having the correct foresight or knowledge on economic issues.

With the current initiatives—both proposed and acted—India will seek to reaffirm its regional leadership in environmental and climate diplomacy as it hosted the first Bay of Bengal Initiative for Multi-Sectoral Technical and Economic Cooperation Disaster Management Exercise (BIMSTEC, DMEx) in 2017 (Ministry of Home Affairs, 2017). It thus, witnesses a major shift in the traditional policy arenas to the holistic new paradigms that BIMSTEC now has been actively engaging in (Parthasarathy, 2017a). The littoral nations of the IOR have been engaged in a highly cooperative mechanism with India as the latter is one of the patrons in the region, adept in disaster response and relief operations. Nations such as Australia and Japan have also concluded bilateral maritime treaties with India in the arenas of connectivity and cooperation.

To offset China's impression across the IOR, strategically and politically, India has arrived at various bilateral and multilateral treaties, involving both regional and extra-regional IOR powers. To avoid the deep-routed piracy of the Indian Ocean high seas, India is engaged in developing many cooperative mechanisms (Borah, 2017). The Kaladan Multimodal Transport Project is one of the most promising road-riverine link that could connect India with its strategic neighbour Myanmar and thereby could act as a land corridor to reach out to the Southeast Asian nations. This 109 kilometre long project pegged at ₹ 1,600 crore (Bose, 2018), once completed, could offer a tough competition to the Belt and Road Initiative of China in the same region. The Maritime India Summit of year 2016, inaugurated by PM Narendra

Modi, observed an overwhelming response through ₹ 83,000 crore investments in the maritime sector.

Submarine building plan of 1999 is the roadmap drawn by Indian Navy to induct 24 submarines by the year 2030. Building a submarine is a complex task that involves 2.5 million person-hours and up to 5 years. INS Kalvarithus becomes the first conventional submarine to join the Indian naval fleet in 17 years. Kalvari, with 1800 tonnes displacement, 36 crew, 300m maximum operating depth, 66m length, 6500nm range, 20 knotes max submerged speed and weaponry like German SUT torpedoes, SM 39 Exocet anti-ship missiles, was commissioned by the Prime Minister of India on December 14, 2017 (Singh, 2017). It is first of the six-scorpene class submarines built at Mazagon Dock Shipbuilders Limited, Mumbai. This submarine is commissioned under Project 75, which is a significant success under the Make in India initiative (Gady, 2017).

But India lags much behind China in naval capacity and it hampers with any big power ambitions that India cherishes. India has 14 diesel electric attack submarines and one nuclear attack submarine Chakra (Akula II) of Russian origin and one ballistic missile submarine Arihant of Indian origin. China has thrice the capacity of India, with 60 diesel electric attack submarines, six nuclear attack and four nuclear ballistic missile submarines (Singh, 2017).

India ought to look at the efficacies of these small Southeast Asian nations such as Malaysia, Philippines and Singapore, which has class-apart ports and shipping companies, which are operational even in the international arena. They have bid for projects within the Indian subcontinents also. On these lines, major ports in India must be forward-looking and use their technical skills to gain strategic objectives. As a strategic partner of the Southeast Asian nations, India had encouraged all claimants to the disputed islands in South China Sea to maintain peace and find a solution within the UNCLOS and ASEAN's Code of Conduct.

While China is building assertive relations in India's neighbourhood, this China-Southeast Asian nations stand-off offers India an opportunity to pursue its 'Act East Policy' with all vigour and might. 'Act East Policy's' maritime dimension thus offers a counterbalancing strategy for India to oppose the encirclement strategy of China.

References

Amador, J.S., Bobillo, A. and Peñalber, A. (2011), "Issues and Challenges in ASEAN-India Relations", *India Quarterly*, 67(2).

Analysis of Criticism against the Proposed PPP at Hambantota Port (2017), *The Daily FT*, April 7, available at: http://www.ft.lk/article/608374/Analysis-of-criticism-against-the-proposed-PPP-at-Hambantota-Port.

Bhatia, R. (2016), "India's Act East Policy and Myanmar's Role", *Distinguished Lectures Detail,* Ministry of External Affairs, available at: http://www.mea.gov.in/distinguished-lectures.htm.

Bilsborough, S. (2013), "China's Emerging C4ISR Revolution", *The Diplomat,* available at: https://thediplomat.com/2013/08/chinas-emerging-c4isr-revolution.

Borah, Rupakjyoti (2017), "India-Myanmar-Thailand Trilateral Highway: A Promise to Transform the Region's Economic Landscape", *Japan Forward*, August 24, available at: https://japan-forward.com/india-myanmar-thailand-trilateral-highway-a-promise-to-transform-the-regions-economic-landscape.

Buckley, C. (2013), "China Leader Affirms Policy on Islands", *The New York Times,* January 29, available at: http://www.nytimes.com/2013/01/30/world/asia/incoming-chinese-leader-will-not-to-bargain-on-disputed-territory.html.

Chakravarty, R. (2017), "India's Changing Global Priorities and the Role of Look East Policy", *Distinguished Lectures Detail*, Ministry of External Affairs, available at: http://www.mea.gov.in/distinguished-lectures.htm.

Dasgupta, S. (2015), "China Says India Must Not Think of Indian Ocean as its Backyard", *The Times of India*, July 1, available at:

https://timesofindia.indiatimes.com/india/China-says-India-must-not-think-of-Indian-Ocean-as-its-backyard/articleshow/47899583.cms.

"Defence Minister Nirmala to Speak on Maritime Threats at Goa Maritime Conclave", *The Times of India,* November 1, 2017, available at: https://timesofindia.indiatimes.com/city/goa/defence-minister-to-speak-on-maritime-threats-at-goa-maritime-conclave/articleshow/61376766.cms.

Gady, F.S. (2017), "India Commissions 1st Kalvari-Class Attack Submarine", *The Diplomat*, December 15, available at: https://thediplomat.com/2017/12/india-commissions-1st-kalvari-class-attack-submarine.

"India-Singapore Joint Naval Exercise SIMBEX 2017 Concludes", *The Economic Times*, May 25, 2017, available at: https://economictimes.indiatimes.com/news/defence/india-singapore-joint-naval-exercise-simbex-2017-concludes/articleshow/58840139.cms.

Jaffrelot, C. (2003), "India's Look East Policy: An Asianist Strategy in Perspective", *India Review*, 2(2).

Jain, B.M. (2017), "India's Security Concerns in the Indian Ocean Region: A Critical Analysis", *Future Directions International*, April 4, available at: http://www.futuredirections.org.au/publication/indias-security-concerns-indian-ocean-region-critical-analysis.

Johnson, K. (2015), "China Tops U.S. as Biggest Oil Importer", *Foreign Policy*, May 11, available at: http://foreignpolicy.com/2015/05/11/china-tops-u-s-as-biggest-oil-importer-middle-east-opec-sloc.

"Joint Media Statement of the Fourth EAS Economic Ministers' Meeting", 2016, available at: http://asean.org/joint-media-statement-of-the-fourth-eas-economic-ministers-meeting.

Kaplan, R. (2009), "Centre-stage for the Twenty-first Century Power Plays in the Indian Ocean", *Foreign Affairs*, 88(2).

Khalid, N. (2012), "Sea Lines under Strain", *IUP Journal of International Relations*, 6(2).

Kohli, S.C. (2016), "Criticism of China-Pakistan Economic Corridor in Pakistan", *Merinews,* December 22, available at:

http://www.merinews.com/article/criticism-of-china-pakistan-economic-corridor-in-pakistan/15921778.shtml.

Kumar, D. (2016), "ASEAN: The Pivot of India's Act East Policy", *The Tribune*, February 11.

Kumar, Y. (2016), "India's Maritime Challenges", *Distinguished Lectures Detail,* Ministry of External Affairs, March 9, available at:
http://www.mea.gov.in/distinguished-lectures-detail.htm?460.

Lockie, A. (2016), How China has Modernized their Navy to Dominate the South China Sea and Beyond", *Business Insider*, June 17, available at:
https://www.businessinsider.in/How-China-has-modernized-their-navy-to-dominate-the-South-China-Sea-and-beyond/articleshow/52799566.cms.

Madhavan, M.C. (2015), "Can India Catch up with China?", *The Hindu,* January 6, available at:
http://www.thehindu.com/opinion/op-ed/comment-can-india-catch-up-with-china/article6757519.ece.

Malik, A.R. and Nunes, W. (2016), "Revisiting Maritime Security in the Indian Ocean", in B.N. Patel, A.K. Malik and W. Nunes (eds.), 'Indian Ocean and Maritime Security: Competition, Cooperation and Threat', New York: Routledge.

Ministry of Home Affairs (2017), "India to Conduct the First BIMSTEC Disaster Management Exercise, 2017 from October 10-13", available at:
http://pib.nic.in/newsite/PrintRelease.aspx?relid=170930.

Ministry of Shipping (2016), "Sagaramala (Building Gateways of Growth): National Perspective Plan.

Mohapatra, P. (2007), "Baliyatra: Reminiscence of Orissa's Maritime Glory", *Orissa Review,* November.

Muni, S.D. (2012), "India's Look East Policy: The Strategic Dimension", in S.M. D'souza and R. Jetly (eds.), 'Perspectives on South Asian Security', Singapore: World Scientific.

Office of Naval Intelligence, "PLA Navy Report", (2015), available at:
https://news.usni.org/2015/04/09/document-office-of-naval-intelligence-2015-assessment-of-chinese-peoples-liberation-army-navy.

Office of Secretary of Defence (2017), "Annual Report to Congress on Military and Security Developments Involving the People's Republic of China", United States of America.

O'Rourke, R. (2017), "China's Naval Modernization: Implications for U.S. Navy Capabilities: Background and Issues for Congress", *Congressional Research Service Report*, December 13.

Parthasarathy, G. (2017a), "It's Time•for India to Revisit Look East", *The Hindu: Business Line*, February 8.

Parthasarathy, G. (2017b), "Dealing with China's Naval Assertiveness", *The Hindu: Business Line,* November 15, available at: http://www.thehindubusinessline.com/opinion/dealing-with-chinas-naval-assertiveness/article9962488.ece.

Pattnaik, J.K. (2017), "Kaladan Multimodal Corridor: A Catalyst for India's North-East", *Mainstream Weekly,* September 9, available at: http://www.mainstreamweekly.net/article7440.html.

Putten, F.D., Wetzling, T. and Kamerling, S. (2014), "Geopolitics and Maritime Security in the Indian Ocean: What Role for the European Union?", The Hague Institute for Global Justice and Clingendael Institute Policy Report, August.

Rolf, S. (2016), "Sovereignty Regimes in the South China Sea: Assessing Contemporary Sino-US Relations", *Eurasian Geography and Economics*, 57(2).

Sahuja, V. (2014), "Indian Ocean: Why India Seeks Demilitarization",. *Institute of Peace and Conflict Studies*, December 15, available at: http://www.ipcs.org/article/india/indian-ocean-why-india-seeks-demilitarisation-4779.html.

Sengupta, J. (2017), "India's Cultural and Civilisational Influence on Southeast Asia", Raisina Debates, Observer Research Foundation, August 30, available at: http://www.orfonline.org/expert-speaks/indias-cultural-and-civilizational-influence-on-southeast-asia.

Singh, D. (2009), "Indo-US Relations", *Strategic Analysis*, 33(6).

Smith, J.M. (2016), "China and Sri Lanka: Between a Dream and a Nightmare", *The Diplomat*, November 18, available at: https://thediplomat.com/2016/11/china-and-sri-lanka-between-a-dream-and-a-nightmare.

Sood, J. (2017), "India Puts Myanmar Highway Project on the Fast Track", *Live Mint*, September 7, available at: http://www.livemint.com/Companies/IPUpgapYWuqhH07OokYWIM/Punj-Llyod-JV-wins-Rs1177-crore-NHAI-project-in-Myanmar.html.

"South China Sea and the Nine-dash Line: What You Need to Know", *The Hindu: International*, July 12, 2016, available at: http://www.thehindu.com/news/international/south-china-sea-and-the-nine-dash-line-what-you-need-to-know/article14485046.ece1.

Tsirbas, M. (2016), "What Does the Nine-Dash Line Actually Mean?", *The Diplomat,* June 2, available at: https://thediplomat.com/2016/06/what-does-the-nine-dash-line-actually-mean.

Wadhwa, A. (2014), "India's Look East-Act East Policy: A Bridge to the Asian Neighbourhood", Distinguished Lecture Detail, Address at the Inaugural Session of the International Relations Conference. Pune, India. December 13, available at: http://www.mea.gov.in/distinguished-lectures.htm.

Wearden, G. (2010), "Chinese Economic Boom has been 30 Years in the Making", *The Guardian*, August 16, available at: https://www.theguardian.com/business/2010/aug/16/chinese-economic-boom.

Yusuf, S. (2018), "China's Belt and Road Gamble: Can it Deliver?", *The SAIS Review of International Affairs*, January 9, available at: http://www.saisreview.org/2018/01/09/chinas-belt-and-road-gamble-can-it-deliver.

Zengerle, P. (2018), "Donald Trump Administration Planning to Cut Pakistan's Security Assistance Aid to Tackle Terror", *The Independent*, January 4, available at: http://www.independent.co.uk/news/world/americas/donald-trump-pakistan-security-assistance-cut-overseas-aid-congress-haqqani-taliban-a8141726.html.

6

Australia's Perception of India's Act East Policy and its Impact on the Region

Sally Burt

This paper is an exploration of India's 'Act East Policy' from an Australian perspective. Australia has great concern for several key issues in the Indo-Pacific region. As the recently released foreign policy White Paper suggests, China's rise and balancing the economic relationship with China and the security alliance with the United States are central to Australia's foreign policy in the region. Australia also has a deep and enduring relationship with India based around the export of tertiary education and the ties created by the large contingent of the Indian Diaspora present in Australia's population. Although the bilateral relationship has not been trouble free in recent times, India is an important partner for Australia in the region, particularly in the context of the rise of China and the balancing of that change in regional dynamics. Australia is seeking to build closer economic ties with India and to cooperate on matters of shared interest such as freedom of navigation in the Indian Ocean, and increasing stability through the region's multilateral organisations. Australia welcomes India's 'Act East Policy' and its increasing involvement in strategic collaboration.

India's ability to balance China's rise and offer a partnership with Australia based on shared democratic values presents significant opportunities for Australia. As competition for power in Asia increases between the US and China, Australia becomes more vulnerable to the outcomes of that contest. India's 'Act East Policy', which is likely to create greater stability in the region by balancing China's rise, is good for Australia. Although Australia will not, in the foreseeable future, turn from the US alliance or from the economic opportunities presented by China, it welcomes the development of bilateral relations with like-minded powers with shared political and economic values, such as India. It also recognises the reduction in vulnerability that comes from the increased interdependence developed in the region by the trade partnerships and multilateral agreements that exist. As such, the friendship between Australia and India is likely to be strengthened as India Acts East and Australia values that friendship deeply.

Introduction

Politics in the Indo-Asia-Pacific region is complex and in a stage of transition that makes policy-making and decisions about the region notoriously difficult. Yet, decisions relating to actions in the region are of paramount importance to those residing and doing business there. India, China and the United States are three key partners for Australia and its relationship with these three ultimately determine the fate of the country. China is Australia's biggest trading partner and it relies on the United States to protect its security interests. Like so many others, Australia must manage within that triangular relationship and balance key interests to make decisions that ultimately keep that triangle from collapsing. As competition for power and influence in the region increases and as China's rise continues, Australia is finding itself at crossroads of policy-making. By expanding its relationship with other key players in the region, such as India, Australia can ensure that it does not become over reliant on China for its economic well-being or mistakenly reliant on the United States to protect its security. India's announcement that it is prepared not only to "Look East" but also to "Act East" presents a welcome opportunity for Australia to engage with another power with significant regional influence.

India-Australia relations have been based for a long time on the exchange of educational opportunities and through the established Indian Diaspora community in Australia. Since midway through the twentieth century, a solid foundation has been laid on which to build a closer and stronger bilateral relationship. Australia and India have increasingly shared interests in the region. There are opportunities to build bilateral relations on an economic basis as well as through increased interaction on the security front. There are also prospects for increased cooperation in multilateral forums and institutions that govern the region.

The most significant issue of common interest is in the protection of freedom of navigation through the waters of the region that are necessary for the increasing volume of trade being conducted in the area. Australia has the ability to supply commodities that are necessary for the continued growth of the Indian economy. India has the ability to provide greater security for the Sea Lines of Communication (SLOCs) in Southeast Asia that are so crucial to Australia's economic prosperity. Canberra has long sought closer ties with India to build the relationship in these ways. Under Prime Minister Modi's leadership and the 'Act East Policy', finally India may requite those advances.

Indo-Australian Relations

Australia has historically had a solid relationship with India based on a set of mutual interests. The supply of education is one significant foundation for the relationship. Indian students have, particularly in recent decades, sought educational opportunities in Australia. In 1951, the Colombo Plan was launched. It was the result of an agreement negotiated at the Commonwealth Foreign Ministers' Conference held in Colombo in January 1950. The Plan provided a framework for countries to provide aid for other Commonwealth countries in Southeast Asia. In the mid-1950s, the focus of Australian aid given through the plan became training and education. Asian students came to Australia and

Australian instructors were sent to different locations in Asia. India was one of the recipient countries of the Colombo Plan.

In the 1990s, the plan was revitalised and its significance for the delivery of aid to the region was noted (Lowe, 2010, pp. 6-10). It was part of an overall awakening in Australia about its role in the region. Since the 1990s, Australia has begun to acknowledge that it is part of Asia and that that requires close interaction within the region. Historical and cultural ties to Britain and Europe shaped Australia's perceptions of itself as a nation and its role in the world. As a result of increased immigration and tourism from Asian nations, as well as the growing globalism and regionalism of the latter part of the twentieth century, Australians are becoming more keenly aware of, and prepared to recognise, the geographic realities of their Asianess (Walker, 2011). India is a 'safe' Asian state to connect with because of the shared history of the Commonwealth experience and English ties.

It is only recently, however, with Narendra Modi's visit to Australia in November 2014, that the two have pursued a security and defence partnership. Australia has long been enthusiastically seeking closer ties with India, but it is really only with the development of the 'Act East Policy' that India has begun to see Australia as a potential security partner in the region (Brewster, 2015). Prime Minister Tony Abbott visited New Delhi in September 2014 following the election of the Modi government several months earlier. As India shows interest in moving away from its commitment to non-alignment, opportunities for cooperation on several key shared interests have arisen (Brewster, 2015). The Abbott government was keen to focus on regional foreign policy and to put regional priorities above wider global interests.

As part of that reshaping of Australian foreign policy, Tony Abbott announced a 100 million dollar new Colombo Plan, and central to that new plan was the creation of educational exchange opportunities (Phillips, 2015). Abbott hoped to build on the traditional foundations of the relationship, being the provision of education, to deepen bilateral ties and expand the security relationship.

Australia has taken a careful approach to the security implications of its uranium exports. Being a good global citizen and signatory to the Nuclear Non-Proliferation Treaty, it has been hesitant to sell uranium to all but the closest of allies and states it can trust to comply with the safeguards agreed to into export agreements. India, along with other parts of Asia has an increasing demand for uranium and exports from Australia are highly sought after in the region. [1] In 2014, Tony Abbott paved the way for exporting uranium to India, justifying the trade through India's commitment to democracy, liberalism, the protection of human rights and the international rule of law (Phillips, 2015).

Australia is also an important supplier of liquid natural gas. This is a commodity of significance to the region, including India. Australia, along with Indonesia, can play a significant role in providing India with energy security in coming decades (Kugelman, 2016). These important commodities can form the basis of a growing trade and economic relationship. Australia is seeking to diversify its trade within the region and India provides an excellent market to expand into. As mentioned above, bilateral relations between Australia and India have been tied to the huge market for education India represents. Education is Australia's second biggest export to India. 60,000 Indians studied in Australia in 2016. Aside from agricultural products and the energy commodities mentioned above, there is also a strong flow of tourists between the two countries that benefits both the economies (DFAT Website). There is, therefore, a solid basis and existing foundation for building a stronger and more prosperous economic and trade relationship.

In Australia's 2017 Foreign Policy White Paper, India was identified as the fastest growing major economy. Australia will seek to benefit from that economic growth and to promote the trade liberalisation necessary to for India to continue in this pattern for decades to come. With a young population by regional standards, India is seen as a good prospect for Australian trade and commerce in the years to come (Australian Government Foreign Policy White Paper, 2017).

The White Paper also identified India as being in the "Front Rank" of Australia's partners in the region. The government is committed to developing a more robust security partnership with India. Maritime security is a key issue for Australia as it depends so heavily on freedom of navigation in the region's waters for trade and economic security. As the economic relationship and trade flows increase between the two countries, this will be an increasingly significant shared interest. Australia was heartened by the Indian government's agreement to hold joint naval exercises in 2015 (Brewster, 2015, p. 41).

Australia will look to work with India on securing the region through the development of governance infrastructure and political organisations that can protect shared interests (Australian Government Foreign Policy White Paper, 2017). Australia sees India as a democratic partner with shared cultural and political values. There is great potential for working together bilaterally and in multilateral forums to protect each other's and shared interests in the region and the globe more generally.

Australia's View of the Rise of China

Australia's relationship with China is complex and is set in a complicated context within the region. China's rise has led to mixed feeling among analysts, scholars and politicians, as well as the general public in Australia. There is a strong sense of fear and apprehension about the threat that China may pose. Insecurity is created by the lack of familiarity with the Chinese state and the lack of intelligence from China about its intentions for the future. On the one hand, Australians want protection from the worst of what China might be capable of in a region it dominates. On the other hand, Australia also wants to benefit from the economic opportunities that China's rising power and economic growth present.

As great power competition heats up in the region and the globe more generally, Australia is inclined to deepen its relationships with as many strategic partners as it can. The scholarship on regional politics suggests that there is a choice to be made between balancing, bandwagoning or hedging when it comes to foreign policy responses to China's rise. [2] Australia is not alone in making this choice. In the last year, however, that choice has been complicated by the lack of clarity about the US's intentions in the region. President Trump has, for the first time, led Australian policymakers to question their ability to rely on the alliance with the US and the future of the security relationship that has been taken for granted for so long. This has also changed Australian perspectives of China.

The majority of Australians, 79 percent according to a recent Lowy Institute opinion poll, accept that trading with China and having access to the Chinese market for exports and imports is vital to Australia's long-term economic interests. Chinese investment in Australia, on the other hand, seems to raise a greater level of anxiety among the Australian public. There is deep scepticism about China's intentions in seeking to purchase Australian agricultural land, residential properties, mining interests and other assets such as ports and facilities for electricity provision that have national security implications (Zongyou, 2015).

Most recently, there have been concerns raised about the level of influence of Chinese officials on Australian Members of Parliament and political parties. The revelation that several key politicians and political parties have received significant donations from prominent Chinese businessmen has sparked fears that Australia's national security has been compromised (McKenzie et al., 2017). The suspicion comes from long held historical views of the Asian races and their desire to "take over" Australia. The longer term development of deeper economic ties, then, may be called into question when Chinese investment is regarded with such distrust. Concerns caused by China's actions in the South China Sea and in other disputes, as well as its plans to increase its military capabilities, have fed a fear of Chinese domination of the region. That fear has led to Australia's search for partners to engage with more closely in order to adopt a hedging strategy (Zongyou, 2015).

As opposed to the views that have led to this hedging strategy, there is an increasing argument made by some scholars that the reality of the global situation is that US power and influence is on the decline. China will inevitably become the biggest global economy and will dominate the Asian region as well as international financial markets. In this new reality, with the United States in retreat from the region and China's taking over, it would make more sense for Australia to acknowledge its position and find ways of dealing with this new reality. [3] By accepting that China will be the new dominant power, Australia could seek alternative policies that allow it to benefit as much as possible from this new reality rather than working against it.

According to this school of thought, time is being wasted fighting the inevitable and damage caused to Sino-Australia relations, as a result of the policies followed to this end will eventually cost Australia in its bilateral relations with China. Policymakers are advised to work with China rather than against it to seek the best outcomes for its own interests and those of the region. These interests need to be redefined in line with this new reality. This would represent a radical departure from long-followed policy platforms. The Australian public and policymakers are some way from accepting this line of argument and making this radical change.

If, however, as some commentators have suggested, the United States has grown tired of providing the security guarantee for so many in the Asian region and the pivot of focus away from the region signalled by President Trump is a more permanent feature of US foreign policy, Australia may have little choice but to strengthen its security relationship with other powers in the region. The Australia-India Framework for Security Cooperation will become a significant aspect of Australia's foreign policy. The framework outlines areas for bilateral cooperation, including in counter-terrorism, border protection, defence technology, disaster management and defence planning and coordination.

As the US withdraws from the region, this Framework could be an important part of Australia's security assurance in the future. The greater hope among Australian policymakers would be that the US will work with India and Australia, as well as Japan to continue to strengthen multilateral security arrangements in the region. Importantly for Australia, China, at almost the same time as the Australia-India Framework for Security Cooperation was announced, concluded a comprehensive trade agreement with Australia. Despite the closer ties with India in the realms of security, China seems undisturbed in its pursuits of closer economic engagement with Australia (Brewester, 2015). If Australia can continue to expand and deepen its security cooperation with India while also developing its economic relationship with China, perhaps it can have the best of both the worlds.

Trilateral Relations: Australia, China and the US

Australia forms part of a diplomatic triangle between it, the US and China. The United States is clearly Australia's biggest ally and it is relied on for the security of Australia's interests in the region. Without the US's weapons and nuclear umbrella, Australia would feel incredibly vulnerable in a region in which it is a middle power and which is volatile and full of competing powers. There are many areas of tension that Australia is not directly involved in but could suffer greatly from the consequences of conflict fought over them. Australian policymakers feel a level of anxiety about having to watch on as bigger players determine the future of the region.

Traditionally, Australia's way of handling this has been to try to create enough influence over events in the region. It has done this by involving itself to the greatest extent possible in the multilateral organisations that govern the region. Australia was a founding member of APEC and has since been heavily involved in its development and its achievements. Australia also recognises the importance of ASEAN and its role in the region and worked to help establish the East Asia Summit which seeks to engage with ASEAN member states to increase dialogue, cooperation and regional integration. [4] Even with the use of multilateral institutions, balancing the bilateral and trilateral relationships with the US and China has been the biggest challenge facing Australia in recent decades and this challenge is unlikely to be resolved in the immediate future.

The level of anxiety about the future has increased during President Trump's time in office. Australia has long regarded itself as a key ally of the United States. The special relationship was reinforced by the Obama Administration's pivot to Asia, which led to increased cooperation between the US and Australia. The stationing of US Marines in Darwin was seen as a clear signal of the US's intentions to protect Australia (along with other allies in the region) from any future threats that may arise. President Trump's treatment of Australia since taking office has led to a rethink of the US's intentions to spend money and political capital in the region for the benefit of its regional allies (White, 2017). Without the security of the United States' defence, Australia can either shift its policies towards bandwagoning with China or hedge further by diversifying its economic and security relationships with other powers in the region, such as India.

In the Rudd-Gillard years, there may have been enough influence in Canberra from those who Hugh White, a China analyst from the Australian National University, calls 'China optimists' for the former to occur (White, 2017). It seems, however, the choice of Prime Minister Turnbull's government has been the latter. Recent events, such as Xi Jinping's election to a second term as Party Chairman without the nomination of a successor as well as the enshrinement of "Xi Jinping Thought" in the Chinese Constitution, actions in the South China Sea and Xi's recent bellicose speech to the military, increases the fears of many in Australia, as well as the region more broadly, about China's intentions for the future of the region.

As mentioned above, Australia has never quite felt a part of the Asian region. Geographically, it fits squarely in the region, but culturally and politically it is clearly a Western power. Having the United States as a key regional player allowed Australia to take some level of comfort in accepting its geographical reality and engaging with the Asian region. In a future Asia without a clear Western power as leader and protector of "Western" interests, Australia would feel even more vulnerable and out of place. This may go some way to explaining why Australia is keen to build its relationship with the closest thing to a Western power the region offers, India. Politicians play up the democratic and Western values that India possesses and use this as a justification for the development of the relationship. China, on the other hand, is Australia's biggest trading partner and the need for access to the Chinese economy for commercial gain and investment is crucial to the health of Australia's economy. Its values, though, are unfamiliar or even contrary to what Australia sees as its values.

For decades, the threat of Communism was a significant cause of fear for Australia and its close relations with the US during the Cold War has meant that that thinking has become very deeply engrained in the Australian psyche. For many years, Australians, along with many others, held out hope that China could be convinced of the folly of their Communist thinking and liberalise to become a more liberal democratic society. Those hopes are hard to maintain under the leadership of Xi Jingping. Changing the Australian psyche to the point where it can accept working with and not against a Communist power will take some time and effort.

India is in a similar position to Australia, in that it has significant relationships with both China and the United States. In fact, many powers in the region find themselves, in the post-Cold War world, in this situation. Having relied on the United States for security guarantees, they are now faced with the economic reality of the growth of the Chinese market and seek to benefit from that relationship while not jeopardising their national security. These two countries represent India's two biggest trading partners. Australia recognises that the development of the relationship between India and the United States and between India and China are of great interest to Australia. [5] There is an opportunity to watch and learn from the way India balances the relationships with these two powers. Australia could even work with India to help keep the United States in the region and develop cooperative relations with China in multilateral forums.

Australia's Perception of India's Act East Policy

Prime Minister Modi's announcement that India was no longer just "Looking East" but also intended to "Act East" was welcomed by the Australian government. India's commitment to ensuring freedom of navigation in regional waters aligns with Australia's interest in keeping regional trade routes and Sea Lines of Communication as open as possible. The Australian government has welcomed the opportunity for deeper engagement with India that the 'Act East Policy' has created. Although Australia has been seeking closer ties for some time, the Modi government has begun to return that advance (Brewster, 2015). It is yet to be seen, however, how much acting East India intends to do. If the new policy is really just a restatement of the 'Look East Policy' and it actually involves little tangible action, Australia will be disappointed.

There is also the problem of who India chooses to act with. Although there has been some interest displayed in building India's relationship with Australia, there are other powers in the region that India has greater interests in working with. That said, there are many mutual benefits to be derived from closer ties between Australia and India. As India's economy continues to grow, it will provide a stable long-term option for Australian investment. The resources Australia has to offer India will assist with that continued economic growth. There are also benefits found in the people-to-people links created between the two countries and the exchange of knowledge and technology resulting from the educational connections. [6]

In Australia's recently released White Paper on Foreign Policy, the nomenclature of Indo-Pacific region was used throughout. This represents a shift away from the rhetoric of the Rudd-Gillard years where the Asian Century and Asian literacy (and China) were a key focus. Although India was included among the key powers in the region that Australia should strengthen its relationship with, the Rudd-Gillard government's policy was clearly focused on drawing closer to China. The "Australia in the Asian Century White Paper" produced in 2012 clearly stated the goal of teaching Asian languages in schools and improving Australian's understanding of Asia. Mandarin was a key focus of the analysis of the paper and the decline in those studying Mandarin from non-Chinese backgrounds was noted as a trend that needed to be reversed (Australia in the Asian Century White Paper, 2012, p. 173).

Prime Minister Kevin Rudd also made significant trips to China and spoke Mandarin in a push to bring Australia and China together. The 2017 Foreign Policy White Paper's use of the Indo-Pacific term is a clear shift away from this Sino-centric thinking. [7] This change in policy represents the different sides of thinking about China that can be found in the Left and Right wings of politics in Australia. Although this divide is not purely along party lines, there is a clear preference for working with China found on the Left and a more cautious and suspicious approach advocated by the Right. In a recent Lowy Institute Opinion Poll, almost half (46 percent) of Australians surveyed opined 'will China become a potential military threat within the next couple of decades'. There has also been a decline in Australians' respect for the US as a result of the Trump Presidency.

A hostile phone call between the US President and Prime Minister Turnbull soon after Trump took office was seen as a serious affront to Australia as a country and a sign that the close alliance relationship was not valued by the Trump Administration. This has led to a decreasing level of trust in the US's intentions to provide Australia with protection in the region (Fullilove and Oliver, 2017). It is in this context that Australia's relationship with India becomes so important. As the only other significant regional player that can challenge China, with the added benefits of being acceptable in terms of Western values and interests, Australia is banking on India balancing China's rise. The 'Act East Policy', then, has positive implications for Australia.

The problem with Acting East and deepening Indian engagement with the region is that it will be a successful policy. That is, as India grows as a great power, it will likely encounter resistance from other powers. It may provoke hostile responses from China and even the US as a result of its success and increasing strength. While India is a more acceptable regional power for Western states because of its democratic values and commitment to a rules-based global order, as it begins to challenge other great powers and act independently of Western or Chinese interests, and even in contradiction to them, India is likely to face increasing challenges from others (Kugelman, 2016).

It is important, then, that India signals benign intentions to the rest of the region so as to make its rise less threatening than China's from foreign perspectives. One way to achieve this is through its use of and engagement with multilateral forums and organisations in the region. By showing that other states' trust in India's democratic and peaceful values is well founded, India will not pose a threat to the status quo in the same way as China and so its rise will be less likely to pose a threat to security and stability in the region. Several key organisations can provide opportunities for India to show its democratic credentials and to reassure other powers in the region of their correctness in hedging with it. One such organisation is ASEAN.

For many decades, ASEAN has been an important focus of Australian foreign relations. As early as the Hawke and Keating Labour governments in Australia in the 1990s, Australia has sought to increase its trade and other interactions with members of the Association (Ravenhill, 1998). In this timeframe, India has also sought closer engagement with ASEAN countries and to use the organisation as a basis for developing more sophisticated bilateral relations with members of the Association (Asher et al., 2001).

China's relations with ASEAN are also in a positive place and this is seen as a stabilising factor in the region. ASEAN's relations with these states do not pose a challenge to the US's influence in the region and they are also seen as drawing China more deeply into the rules-based system the US is so keen to maintain in the region (Storey, 2007). ASEAN can be seen, then, as a significant factor in the regional interaction of many powers and may hold the key for engagement into the future. It may also provide the impetus for the economic reforms necessary for continuing strong growth in the Indian economy. ASEAN will also provide assistance in the maritime space and its joint interest in protecting SLOCs and maritime trade mean that Australia also shares an interest in improving its own relations with ASEAN, but also bilateral relations between ASEAN and India and ASEAN and China (Bhattacharya, 2007).

Conclusion

Australia's recently released White Paper on Foreign Policy is clear in its vision for the future of the Indo-Pacific region. It shows that Australia is not ready to give up on the idea of the US maintaining a strong security presence in the region that will protect its interests in the future. It also shows the different sides of the foreign policy debate occurring in Australia at the moment. Both sides acknowledge Australia's dependence on its economic relationship with China and its reliance on its alliance with the United States for security protection. The two uncertainties that determine the approach advocated by scholars and foreign policy experts are the future intentions of China and the US in the region. The Trump Administration has shown that for the duration of its time in office, Obama's pivot to Asia is a thing of the past. Trump has not only signalled that he wants the US to rethink its allocation of resources to the region.

More worryingly for Australia is that he has also signalled that he is not as supportive of the ANZUS Treaty relationship as previous presidents have been. His first phone call with Prime Minister Malcolm Turnbull was hostile and along with other comments and policies Trump has made, has resulted in a decline in Australia's respect and thinking about the United States. If this turn away from Asia is an aberration, then Australia will do well to ride out the storm of the Trump Presidency and hold on to its traditional alliance thinking that the US will provide it with security in the region and so the close friendship should be maintained. If, on the other hand, the withdrawal is a more permanent feature of the US's long-term strategy for the region, then Australia needs to rethink its security arrangements and look for other suitable partners with whom it can create and maintain defence ties.

China's intentions in the region would also create uncertainty for Australian policymakers. There are some in Australia who believe that China will be an economic powerhouse and is likely to do little that will upset the balance of the rules-based order that provides the foundations for its economic growth. Australia, therefore, has little to fear from China and should aim to derive as many economic benefits as it can from that growth. Australia should take advantage of Chinese investment and its markets to trade as much as possible.

According to this thinking, Australians should also aim to become more accepting of Asian culture and seek to understand China and other Asian nations more fully so as to be able to operate in the region with China as the economic lead. Another school of thought is that China has hostile long-term intentions for the region and is likely to pose a military threat to Australia and the region in the coming decades. In this case, Australia is best to seek economic opportunities elsewhere so as not to become overly dependent on trade and investment with China in order to achieve its own economic prosperity. By diversifying trade relationships in the region, Australia can protect its economy and society from the worst effects of a hostile China in years to come.

Although under the Rudd-Gillard government, Australia was leaning towards China and trying to become more Asian literate so as to operate with China in greater cooperation, under the Abbott-Turnbull government it has turned the other way. Australia is seeking a broader security framework in the region to hedge against a pattern begun under President Trump of disengagement with Asia. Much more comfortable with the Obama Administration's pivot to Asia, the Australian government shows signs of concern about the direction of US foreign policy in the future.

Australia has also sought to diversify its economic relationships with growing economies in the region to decrease its reliance on China. India has the potential to be a solid economic partner for Australia with opportunities for mutual benefits from trade and investment and also to work with Australia in the area of defence and security. Australia and India have a good historic relationship based on common interests and shared values. India's 'Act East Policy', then, is very much welcomed by the Australian government who has been seeking closer bilateral relations for some time. If India is willing to build the relationship and expand the basis of cooperation and collaboration in the region, Australia is happy to reciprocate. India is a strong regional power and also an acceptable cultural partner for Australia. By focusing on India's democratic values and its support for the continuation of a rules-based global order and commitment to maintaining oceanic interactions regulated by the United Nations Convention on the Law of the Sea, Australia can fully support deeper engagement with India.

Closer India-Australian bilateral relations are a good hedging bet. Even if China's intentions prove to be benign and it does not pose a military threat to Australia and the region in the future, it seems that Australia and India drawing closer does not concern China, at least at the moment. So, Australia would not lose anything if it does not aggravate the Chinese by working with India.

If the United States also decides to return its pivot to Asia in a post-Trump world, again, Australia has lost nothing as India and the US have sought closer collaboration in the region in the past. India is a good balancer to China and those with interests in the stability of the region will work with India to support that balance. India poses none of the threats of China and lack the uncertainty of US policy in the future. Until the intentions of the two biggest players in the region, and the outcome of their competition becomes clear, it is prudent for Australia to work against the worst case scenario and protect itself from the worst outcomes as best it can. Perhaps, if Australia can maintain relations with China, India and the United States, it will have successfully fulfilled the hopes of the New Colombo Plan.

Notes

1. http://www.world-nuclear.org/information-library/country-profiles/countries-a-f/australia.aspx.
2. See, for example, Evelyn Goh (2013), "The Struggle for Order: Hegemony, Hierarchy and Transition in Post-Cold War East Asia", Oxford: Oxford University Press.
3. See, for example, Hugh White (2017), "Without America: Australia in the New Asia", in *Quarterly Essay*, Issue 68, pp. 1-

81; Malcolm Fraser, "American: Australia's Dangerous Ally" in *The National Interest*, December 16, 2014, available at: http://nationalinterest.org/feature/america-australias-dangerous-ally-11858; and
Richard Fontaine (2016), "Against Complacency: Risks and Opportunities for the Australia-US Alliance", The United States Studies Centre, University of Sydney, October.

4. These are only some examples of Australia's work in regional forums. See, the Australian Government's Department of Foreign Affairs and Trade Website on regional architecture, available at:
http://dfat.gov.au/international-relations/regional-architecture/apec/Pages/asia-pacific-economic-cooperation-apec.aspx.
5. Joint Statement by Prime Minister Turnbull and Prime Minister Modi, visit to India, April 10, 2017, Australian Department of Foreign Affairs and Trade website, available at:
http://dfat.gov.au/geo/india/Pages/joint-statement-by-prime-minister-turnbull-and-prime-minister-modi-visit-to-india-2017.
6. Joint Statement by Prime Minister Turnbull and Prime Minister Modi, visit to India, April 10, 2017, Australian Department of Foreign Affairs and Trade website, available at:
http://dfat.gov.au/geo/india/Pages/joint-statement-by-prime-minister-turnbull-and-prime-minister-modi-visit-to-india-2017.
7. Although the term "Indo-Pacific" was commonly used in the 2013 Defence White Paper, it is almost absent from the 2012 Australia in the Asian Century White Paper, showing that although the defence establishment had begun a shift in its strategic thinking, the government was still thinking politically about the Asia-Pacific.

References

Asher, Mukul, et al. (2001), "ASEAN-India: Emerging Economic Opportunities", paper prepared for ASEAN-INDIA workshop on Economic Issues organized by the French centre de Sciences Humaines, Institute of Southeast Asian Studies, Singapore, and School of International Studies, Jawaharlal Nehru University, New Delhi, March 17-18.

Australian Government, Department of Defence, "Australia in the Asian Century White Paper", 2012, available at:

http://www.defence.gov.au/whitepaper/2013/docs/australia_in_the_asian_century_white_paper.pdf.

Australian Government, Department of Foreign Affairs and Trade, "Australian Foreign Policy White Paper", 2017, available at: https://www.fpwhitepaper.gov.au.

Bhattacharya, Anushree (2007), "India's Joint Naval Exercises in the ASEAN Region" Institute of Peace and Conflict Studies #2345, August 3, available at: www.ipcs.org/article_details.php?articleNo=2345.

Brewster, David, "The Australia-India Framework for Security Cooperation: Another Step towards an Indo-Pacific Security Partnership", *Security Challenges*, Vol. 11, No.1, pp. 39-48.

Fontaine, Richard (2016), "Against Complacency: Risks and Opportunities for the Australia-US Alliance", The United States Studies Centre, University of Sydney, October.

Fraser, Malcolm (2014), "American: Australia's Dangerous Ally", *The National Interest,* December 16, available at: http://nationalinterest.org/feature/america-australias-dangerous-ally-11858.

Fullilove, Michael and Alex Oliver (2017), "Almost Half of Us Fear China Could Become a Threat", Commentary by the Lowy Institute, June 21, available at: https://www.lowyinstitute.org/publications/almost-half-us-fear-china-could-become-threat-0.

Goh, Evelyn (2013), "The Struggle for Order: Hegemony, Hierarchy and Transition in Post-Cold War East Asia", Oxford: Oxford University Press.

India Country Brief, Department of Foreign Affairs and Trade website, available at: http://dfat.gov.au/geo/india.

Joint Statement by Prime Minister Turnbull and Prime Minister Modi, visit to India, April 10, 2017, Australian Department of Foreign Affairs and Trade website, available at: http://dfat.gov.au/geo/india/Pages/joint-statement-by-prime-minister-turnbull-and-prime-minister-modi-visit-to-india-2017.

Kugelman, Michael (2016), "India Acts East", *The South Asia Channel*, May 17.

Lowe, David (2010), "The Colombo Plan and 'Soft' Regionalism in the Asia-Pacific: Australian and New Zealand Cultural

Diplomacy in the 1950s and 1960s", Alfred Deakin Research Institute Working Paper, Geelong, pp. 6-19.

McKenzie, Nick, et al., "China's Operation Australia", *Sydney Morning Herald*, available at: http://www.smh.com.au/interactive/2017/chinas-operation-australia/hard-power.html.

Phillips, Andrew (2015), "Issues in Australian Foreign Policy: July to December 2014", *Australian Journal of Politics and History*, Vol. 61, No. 2, pp. 263-277.

Ravenhill, John (1998), "Adjusting to the ASEAN Way: Thirty Years of Australia's Relations with ASEAN", *The Pacific Review*, Volume 11, Issue 2, pp. 267-289.

Storey, Ian (2007), "The United States and ASEAN-China Relations: All Quiet on the Southeast Asia Front", Strategic Studies Institute, Carlisle PA.

Walker, David (2011), "Naming and Locating Asia: Australian Dilemmas in its Regional Identity, in Alterities in Asia: Reflections on Identity and Regionalism", London: Routledge.

White, Hugh (2017), "Without America: Australia in the New Asia", *Quarterly Essay*, Issue 68, pp. 1-81.

Zongyou, Wei (2015), "Australia's Strategic Perceptions of China: Hedging or Balancing?", *China International Studies*, July/August, pp. 100-114.

7

Japan in India's Act East Policy: Confluence of Interests and Strategy

Anil Kumar P.

India's metamorphosis as an Asian-engaged nation regained its momentum with the declaration of 'Look East Policy' in 1992, which launched India's efforts to cultivate extensive economic and later strategic relations across Southeast Asia and then the wider Asia-Pacific region. It led India to pursue economic modernisation and integration into the capitalist trade and finance framework and to expanded strategic interactions designed to establish its status as a regional and international power. The historical connections, rich cultural bondage and convergence of economic, strategic and geopolitical interests in the post-Cold War period made Japan the natural ally of India in its 'Look East' to 'Act East Policy'.

The rise of China, India's 'Act East Policy' in conjunction with US Asia Pivot policy, aggressive Chinese maritime moves and their One Belt One Road Initiative, the diffused global focus of US and their strengthening relationship with India and convergence of maritime, security and economic interests in the Asia-Pacific region constitute the context that elevate India-Japan relations to the level of 'global partnership'. The transformation of the security environment in the Southeast Asian region exhibits an "order transition" rather than a "power transition" [1] and the rise of India-Japan relation is consequential not only because they are maritime powers but also because it exhibits a shift in US alliance politics in the region from a bilateral-based one to a multilateral security network.

India wants to transform its ASEAN-centric 'Look East' policy into an 'Act East' policy that seeks to assert its presence in various parts of Asia from Myanmar to Japan and Australia and the two Oceans. Maintenance of balance of power vis-à-vis China is not the sole driver of these bilateral relations. A closer examination of the China factor in India-Japan relations reveals that purely realist balance of power concerns will not reflect the whole aspects. The other side of the coin reveals that both Tokyo and New Delhi are cautious, aware and sensitive not to be abrasive in their respective equations with China. These countries are therefore choosing to hedge and practice *soft balancing* against the potentially precipitous fallout of Beijing's rise in case it gets threatening.

There are other forces like functional need, inter-dependence and simply the prospects of mutual gain, which shape relations between the two sides, even though these have not been fully realised and exploited. The *securitization* and *de-securitization* processes in the region have also resulted in the convergence of interests between Southeast Asian states and the participation of extra-regional states like Japan and India. Indo-Japanese strategic and defence relationship is construed as a vital complement for Washington's current regional security. This paper is basically locating Japan in India's 'Act East Policy' and discusses how the convergence of economic, strategic and geopolitical interests of Japan and India make them crucial allies in the context of the transformations in Southeast Asia. It also attempts to analyse the efforts of India and Japan to move beyond the Association of South East Asian Nations (ASEAN) region through the framework of 'minilateralism' of quads and triangles.

India and Japan: Confluence of Interests

The rise of China and the power shift in Asia becomes a primary factor in bringing Tokyo and New Delhi together. But there are many factors which are cementing India-Japan relations in this 21st century. Maintenance of balance of power vis-à-vis China is not the sole driver of foreign policy and bilateral relations between India and Japan. There are other forces like functional need, inter-dependence and the prospects of mutual gain. Historically, India-Japan relations have existed for more than a thousand years. It is said that Japan first came into contact with India during the reign of Emperor Kimmei (539-571 A.D.). [2]

Buddhism was the first common link between both the sides, although it did not really find its way directly between the two countries. Another vital connection between both the sides was a result of the common feeling of Pan-Asianism. During the period of the Indian Renaissance (1881-1905), India was keenly looking at building a spirit of Asian oneness. Organisations like Oriental Youngman's Association formed in 1900 served as a platform for increased interaction between Japanese, Indian and other Asian students in Japan.

Despite Japan's aloofness with the rest of the world, the connectivity between India and Japan remained with the fast-growing Japanese spinning industry, which found India as a source of raw cotton. India also became a destination for finished Japanese goods. Perhaps the most significant bilateral contact was that of Indian industrialist J.N. Tata who visited Japan in 1893 and set up an office there. The initiation of trade ties led to the establishment of a Japanese consulate office in Bombay and consulate general office in Calcutta. [3] An Indo-Japanese Trade convention was also signed in 1894 which marked the beginning of "opening of regular ocean transport" between the two sides. [4]

After its war with Russia, Japan becomes a role model for Indians to fight against colonialism. The formation of *Indo-Japan Friendship Association* (1903), *Indian Club* (1921), India's affinity towards Japan even in the midst of *Swadeshi Movement* [5] and the role played by Indian revolutionaries like Rash Bihari Bose and Subhash Chandra Bose [6] are very important in creating intimate links with Japan and the Japanese. On the cultural and literary front, the legendary friendship between

Okakura Tenshin and Indian poet Rabindranath Tagore accelerated this process. But with Japan's militarisation and imperialist lash-out in the 1930s, relations between India and Japan began to deteriorate. Japan's advancement into China—the Manchurian Incident, its actions in Korea (1910-1911) eroded the positivity which defined and underlined bilateral relations between both sides. Attempt for a good friendship and Nehru's interest give a new impetus to India-Japan relations with the signing of the bilateral treaty of 1952.

The distance between India and Japan grew wider during the time of Cold War. India, despite choosing to follow a policy of non-alignment, had a definitive tilt towards the former Soviet Union. Japan, on the other hand, had become an ally of the United States, placing both sides in opposite camps. In addition to this, India's nuclear tests in 1974 become a huge shock for Japan. South Asia was largely a "distant region" for Japan till the late 1990s and did not fall within its definition of the Asia-Pacific or Asia. Historically, India and Japan shared much in terms of religion and culture, which should have ideally provided enough bedrock for a stable superstructure of relationships. There were a number of potential binding factors which could glue the two sides more effectively than they did.

Japan had an important indirect participatory role in the Indian National Movement. However, the post-war period was underscored by a chill in relations which summed up to be a considerable loss for both sides in terms of opportunities which they could have possibly built upon.

Post-Cold War Scenario

Japan's strategic thinking changed a lot in the post-Cold War period in the midst of the Gulf War. It became a milestone in Tokyo's strategic thinking as it came under censure from Washington over its inability to contribute manpower to assist its ally. Despite making a significant contribution to the tune of US$ 13 billion, Japan was criticised for mere "chequebook diplomacy". Other developments which shook up Japan were the North Korean missile tests in 1993, the U.S.-North Korean nuclear crisis in 1994 and firing of Pyongyang's missile which flew over Japan's Honshu island in 1998. The rise of China during this decade also became a challenge for the region and actors therein—including India and Japan. What is obviously and lucidly apparent is the common concern over China's growing assertion, rapid military modernization, claims and conflict over territory and arms build-up which had begun sprouting during this period and continues unabated till today.

India-Japan relations began to change in the early 1990s with launching of India's 'Look East Policy' in 1991, liberalisation of the economy, and the international situation of Post-Cold War period. As bemoaned by former Foreign Secretary J. N. Dixit, "Japan was identified as one of the most important sources of both investment and technology by the Government of India". [7] But the nuclear tests of India in 1998 had a negative impact on India-Japan relations. But Delhi's announcement of having a moratorium on conducting further tests revoked the position of the bilateral relationship on a positive track.

However, major changes began to reflect in the bilateral ties only in 2000 with the historic visit of Japanese Prime Minister Mori Yoshiro to India in August, marking a new chapter in relationship. The relations between India and Japan got fresh impetus going beyond economic and trade relations with gradual improvement in US-India relations and the signing of the US-India nuclear deal in 2005. Several factors including China's rise and other security concerns such as maritime security have influenced the changing nature of the relations between the two. Even though the initial rationale for this eastward foray by India was economic, strategic imperatives also played a significant role in it.

For India, Southeast and East Asian countries provide an avenue not just for economic integration but also strategic linkages. New Delhi has had increased defence exchanges, joint exercises, joint patrolling of sea lanes of communication and dialogues between security establishments of both the sides. This was India's response to what it viewed as China's challenge to its interests in the Indian Ocean. For instance, the Indian Navy was called upon to participate in a multinational navy exercise in the Philippines named "Team Challenge" in 2002 involving Australia, Brunei, Indonesia, Japan, Korea, Malaysia and Singapore among others. What was significant was the fact that it was the first-ever exercise by the Indian Navy in the East Asian security region. [8]

Similarly, India conducted joint passage exercises with the Japanese Maritime Self Defence Force in the East China Sea in October 2008. [9] The Malabar 2007 exercises, which also included trilateral exercises between the United States, Japan and India, were also a landmark event. The "extended neighbourhood" formulation encompassed both southeast and northeast Asia as well. China's economic threat, military modernization and converging demands and issues of India and Japan became a booster to bilateral relationship between them. The recognition of India's emergence as an economic powerhouse became evident. In a Yomiuri Shimbun poll taken in July 2006, as many as 20 percent of Japanese chose India as the third most important country in the future of world economy after China and the United States. [10]

The warming up of Washington's relations with New Delhi especially since the late 1990s also led Japan to take a more positive note of India. The 2002 U.S. National Security Strategy called for close ties with India for a "strategically stable Asia". [11] Besides, there seemed to be some realisation trickling in Japanese strategic community on the ability of India's nuclear status to balance China in some way. The terrorist attacks in the United States also kindled the Japanese urge to assist India and the region in its combat against terrorism.

First, Japan started recognising the advantages of bringing New Delhi in its fold especially in inter-government institutions mushrooming in the region. There is a certain realisation between both sides that they share a number of areas of common concern. There is, therefore, a resultant co-operation in areas including safety and security of sea lanes of communication and a permanent seat in the UN Security Council.

Second, there are economic complementarities between both countries with India's human resource capital and manpower complementing Japanese "money power" and technical prowess. Japan's ageing society is a severe problem today and the country lacks young and active workforce. India's abundant cheap and skilled workforce can make up for this gap.

Third is the oft-mentioned value based connectivity—democracy, freedom and human rights which combine with rich cultural and historical links. The legacy of history has perhaps become the most important variable which continues to connect Japan's ties with most of its Asian neighbours. Tokyo has had problems with Asian neighbours like China and South Korea over the history issue with offshoots in the Yasukuni Shrine issue, the textbooks issue and differing positions over the Nanjing "massacre" and wartime history. The fact that there is no such historical irritant with India makes it easier for the two sides to work towards building the relationship further. A positive public opinion has only bolstered bilateral relations between India and Japan.

For India, Japan is a critical source of capital and commercial technology. Indeed, there cannot be a better partner for India's development than the country that was the first non-western society to modernise and emerge as a world power, spearheading Asia's industrial and technological advances since the 19th century. India has underscored the importance of also building security collaboration with it, saying Indians "see Japan as a natural and indispensable partner in our quest for stability and peace in the vast" Indo-Pacific region.

Japan and India, as energy-poor countries heavily reliant on oil imports from the unstable Persian Gulf region, are seriously concerned over mercantilist efforts to assert control over energy supplies and the transport routes for them. So the maintenance of a peaceful and lawful maritime domain, including unimpeded freedom of navigation, is critical to their security and economic well-being. That is why they have moved from emphasising shared values to seeking to protect shared interests, including by holding joint naval exercises. Japanese and Southeast Asian investors consider India as a potential location for their export-oriented investments as a hedge against their perceived over-dependence on China. India offers a large domestic market, industrial depth, urban centres, and sophisticated financial services.

India and Japan boast of the fastest-growing bilateral relationship in Asia today. Since they unveiled a "strategic and global partnership" in 2006, their political and economic engagement has deepened at a remarkable pace. Their free-trade pact, formally known as the Comprehensive Economic Partnership Agreement (CEPA), came into force in 2011. They have even established an alliance to jointly develop rare-earth minerals so as to reduce their dependence on China. The level and frequency of India-Japan official engagement have become extraordinary. In addition to holding an annual Prime Minister-level summit, the two also conduct several yearly ministerial dialogues: A strategic dialogue between their Foreign Ministers; a security dialogue between their Defence Ministers; a policy dialogue between India's Commerce Minister and Japan's Minister of Economy, Trade and Industry; and separate ministerial-level energy and economic dialogues. And, to top it off, they also hold a trilateral strategic dialogue with the United States.

Strategic Ties in the Modi Era

Today, the confluence of Modinomics and Abenomics is now a common refrain. They (Modi and Japanese Prime Minister Shinzo Abe) are decisive leaders aiming at accelerating faltering growth momentum. This is evident during the maiden visit of Indian Prime Minister Narendra

Modi to Japan in September 2014, which has been touted as the crown jewel in India's East Asia diplomacy. New Delhi not only secured unprecedented economic investment from Tokyo but also found a partner for economic growth. India's need for a financial boost for its economy cannot be overstated and the trip has clearly bolstered bilateral ties. To realize its full economic and demographic potential, India needs a partner that can provide multi-sector support. Modi and Abe went further, discussing their nascent military engagements, triggering speculation over a gradually solidifying Indo-Japanese strategic alliance, particularly through the prism of the "China threat". [12]

Modi attached great importance to the annual summit meetings with Japan during his first term, and between 2014 and 2018 there were five summit meetings held alternately between Tokyo and Delhi. Modi's 2014 visit was followed by visits in 2016 and 2018. Similarly, Abe visited India in 2015 and 2017. The very first meeting held in Tokyo set the tone by issuing the Tokyo Declaration, which elevated bilateral ties to a special 'Strategic and Global Partnership'. Emphasising the need for closer coordination between the two countries to address regional security challenges, Modi has supported robust defence cooperation with Japan.

Such co-operation has been expanding in recent years and is buttressed by the regular Annual Strategic Dialogue between the two Foreign Ministers and the Defence Dialogue between the two Defence ministers. In addition, there have been regular exchange visits by the respective Service Chiefs as well as the two National Security Advisers. Further, at the 2018 summit, Modi and Abe agreed to create a new Foreign and Defence Ministerial Dialogue to further strengthen defence co-operation. [13] In addition, Modi has elevated the US-India-Japan trilateral dialogue to the ministerial level. There is also greater coordination between India, Japan, the US, and Australia under the QUAD format.

With regard to China, both Modi and Abe share concerns on a range of issues including the future role of China in the Indo-Pacific region, Beijing's assertive maritime postures in the Indian Ocean, and its Belt and Road Initiative. At a time when the Indo-Pacific region is faced with critical strategic challenges, both leaders have maintained a policy of engaging with Beijing. They are realistic enough to understand that in any future regional strategic scenario, because of its economic and military strength, China will figure quite prominently. It is therefore necessary to ensure that the rise of China takes place without disturbing the prevailing regional equilibrium. Interests of both India and Japan will be best served if the Indo-Pacific region remains multipolar with no single regional power assuming a preponderant position. [14]

In their first bilateral summit held in Tokyo, both Modi and Abe set the target of doubling Japan's direct investment and the number of Japanese private companies in India. Japan agreed to extend US$ 33.5 billion public and private investment in India apart from funding from the Official Development Assistance (ODA) over five years. This amount would be used to support projects in several areas including infrastructure, connectivity, transport, smart cities, energy, and skill development. Modi decided to set up a number of industrial townships and electronic parks for developing technology, connecting people, and inspiring innovation. In turn, Abe affirmed that Japan would support India's 'Make-in India', 'Digital India' and 'Skill India' programmes.

Between 2014 and 2018, the amount and quality of Japan's ODA as well as Japanese private investment witnessed appreciable improvement. India remained on top of the list of ODA recipients and the economy gained numerous benefits from Japan's ODA loans, which flowed into many critical sectors like power, transportation, communication, environment, water, public health, and agriculture. The quantum of Japanese investment increased from US$ 1.7 billion in 2014 to US$ 4.7 billion in 2016-17. [15] With a cumulative foreign direct investment (FDI) of US$ 25.2 billion from April 2000 to December 2016, Japan is the third largest investor in India—accounting for eight percent of India's total FDI. Japanese investment has flowed into the automobile, telecommunication, chemical and pharmaceutical sectors.

Modi has, from the beginning, emphasised the importance of India's North-East Region (NER) in his "Act East Policy". He has taken a special interest in Japan playing a key role in the development of the NER. Modi and Abe established the India-Japan Act East Forum, which will provide a platform for bilateral collaboration and identify projects for economic and social development of the region. [16] Both leaders consider the NER as a critical region, where India's 'Act East Policy' and Japan's "Free and Open Indo-Pacific Strategy" converge, and both countries are keen to extend their cooperation to the larger Indo-Pacific region—including the African continent. In May 2016, Modi announced a proposal to develop an Asia-Africa Growth Corridor with the support of Japan. [17]

This proposal is aimed at creating a "free and open Indo-Pacific region" by building a series of sea corridors that would connect the African continent with India and other countries of South and Southeast Asia. One important objective is to bring about greater integration within the Indo-Pacific region by undertaking several infrastructure projects. India and Japan have already started collaborating on projects in Myanmar, Sri Lanka, Bangladesh, and Kenya to this end.

All the above mentioned factors solidify the argument that India-Japan relations are reaching unprecedented heights due to the international compulsions, common concerns and shared strategic interests.

Japan in India's Act East Policy

The history of India's engagement with Southeast Asia was rich during Nehru's period. But the Cold War and the ideological differences kept the relations under cold storage. Later, 'Look East Policy' had officially begun under

Narasimha Rao government in the early 1990s. This occurred in the context of economic recession in India which had compelled India to open up its markets and undertake structural reforms that pushed India in search for economic opportunities with newly emerged tiger economies of ASEAN. Historically speaking, S.D. Muni calls it "fourth wave" of India's 'Look East' that was formally launched by Prime Minister Narasimha Rao in his famous September 1994 lecture in Singapore though it owed a lot to his predecessor's (Rajiv Gandhi) efforts from mid-1980s especially latter's official visits to Indonesia and Thailand during October 1986. [18]

Soon after taking over as India's Foreign Minister, during her first visit to Vietnam in August 2014, Sushma Swaraj was to enunciate this policy as she outlined Prime Minister Narendra Modi's vision to give boost to India's 'Look East Policy', turning it into "an Act East Policy" of India. [19] This is not a simple upgrading of the 'Look East Policy' as India seems to clearly indicate its readiness to play a far more active and prominent role in the region and this has since translated into India's enhanced diplomatic footwork across East and Southeast Asia. [20] India's East Asia policy is now being seen clearly in two phases: first 'Look East' since 1992; and from 2014, in its reincarnation as India's 'Act East' policy seeking deeper strategic engagement in connectivity, culture and commerce. Modi's 'Act East Policy' transformed India's ASEAN centric policy to beyond ASEAN and it started to work through the QUADS—US, Japan, Australia and India.

The method of working through quads and triangles has been seen as an effective mechanism in literature on global governance which calls it 'minilateralism' that was originally popularised by Miles Kahler in early 1990s and revived in 2009 by Moises Naim and Thomas Wright in their highly debated article respectively in *Foreign Policy* and *Washington Quarterly*. [21] Naim, in particular, points out that minilateralism is a smarter approach because it is more targeted and has the largest possible impact on solving a specific problem. Using this potent mechanism, India and Japan have not only been in spotlight for their expanding co-operation but also how these have contributed to New Delhi's visualization of 'Act East Policy' that seeks to add vigour and substance to India's extant engagement with East Asian countries.

The efficacy of India's engagement with Japan has also created expectations in the United States and amongst its friends and allies who see India as their would-be counterweight to China's rising influence. [22] It is partly in "channelling their frustrations" and expectations that Secretary of State Hilary Clinton, during her visit to India way back in 2011 had said: "We encourage India not just to look East, but to engage East and to act East as well". [23] New Delhi has taken substantial steps towards the United States and its Asian allies which have "transformed India's relationship with Japan into a robust strategic partnership with substantial efforts in maritime cooperation".

In making India welcome in East Asia, Japan has also not only been a friendly voice in all the multilateral forums where both these are members but India and Japan have worked closely in several 'minilateral' forums like the Quad of Democracies (US, Japan, Australia, India) and Triangular Ministerial Dialogue (of US, Japan, India) as also as their recently revived quad of the G4 (of Germany, Japan, Brazil, India) which seeks UN reforms and permanent seats for them in the UN Security Council.

At the trilateral level, the cooperation between the US, India and Japan was established primarily to maintain maritime security. The challenges for developing this trilateral dialogue further included the burden of public opinion with regard to history of Japanese militarism, while Indian politicians believed there was "mileage to be gained from anti-American posturing". The US, in addition had also been reticent about Japan's emergence as military power.

In spite of these challenges, the last trilateral dialogue held in June 2015 discussed the US rebalance to Asia, India's 'Act East Policy' and Japan's more active security role. This momentum of increased convergent interests has since enabled then to upgrade this dialogue 'to the ministerial level in September 2015, which was followed in the 5-day joint naval exercise in October in the off coast of the Bay of Bengal. The exercise Malabar included one of the world's largest carriers, the US Theodore Roosevelt as well as the US missile cruiser and a nuclear-powered submarine and included Japan as permanent member of these exercises.

In fact, the post-2011 US discourses on rebalance and 'pivot' to Asia, accompanied by US and Australia propping the new Indo-Pacific geopolitical framework, has been accompanied by post-2013 Chinese discourses on One Belt One Road Initiative that seeks to connect western Pacific to Baltic Sea through building infrastructure projects for connectivity and commerce. This has left the Japanese often far too uncertain on whether they still are on the same page with regards to US visions on how to develop their shared security strategies for East Asia. In 2012, US National Defence Strategic Guidance, had stated that "U.S. economic and security interests are inextricably linked to developments in the arc extending from the Western Pacific and East Asia into the Indian Ocean region and South Asia, creating a mix of evolving challenges and opportunities". [24]

Experts increasingly are reading India's 'Act East' policy and US 'Pivot to Asia' as being largely reciprocal and focussed on their shared concerns about Chinese. [25] What makes US support to India's 'Act East Policy' promising is the bipartisan support (indeed enthusiasm) for it in the U.S. and both sides see this in conjunction with their own policy objectives. [26] But most such headlines driven commentaries often miss the point that though such inflections of the U.S. global leadership are precious, these are relatively symbolic compared to solid cooperation amongst those sitting on

China's periphery and especially those who feel directly threatened by China's rise and even see possibilities of existential threats from it.

This makes Japan a natural partner for India's 'Act East Policy' in not just dealing with China's rise but also in seeking to mould larger Asian decision-making through norm-entrepreneurship and consensus building as basis for regional good governance. India's 'Act East Policy' aims to achieve precisely this and Japan has not only been India's strongest pillar of seeking this expanded engagement but promises to remain a critical interlocutor in India's increasing acceptance and participation in building peace and stability across East Asia. This change can be narrated as an "order" transition rather than a "power" transition in the region.

Act East: Reflection of an *Order* Transition

The strengthened relationship between Delhi and Tokyo reflects a maturing, multilateral security collaboration between the United States, India, and Japan. Japan and India—both hesitant in the use of force since 1945—are emerging as proactive players in the realm of international security with an articulate identity as maritime powers and a sense of internationalism. [27] The emergence of these formerly reluctant major powers reveals that the transformation of the security environment in the region exhibits an "order transition" rather than a "power transition", where China simply takes over America's preponderance position. The rise of these powers is consequential not only because they are maritime powers but also because it exhibits a shift in US alliance politics in the region from a bilateral-based one to a multilateral security network.

While the changes in Japan and India's security policies are informed by balancing behaviour towards China, the resurgence and collaboration of these two powers reveal an intricate and profound transformation of the international order. The increasingly destabilising security environment in the region, particularly in the maritime domain, has triggered fears of a major confrontation. A popular focus on the rise of China, associated with speculations over the relative decline of the US, triggered debates over a possible "power transition" in the region, where Beijing replaces Washington's preponderance position in the Indo-Pacific. On the contrary, the rise of India and Japan rather implies an "order transition", which has occurred steadily since the end of the Cold War.

The emerging partnership between India and Japan is the rise of internationalism in both capitals, a developing identity as maritime states and also the evolution of the US-led alliance system in the Indo-Pacific. [28] China's increasingly assertive behaviour is a definite trigger. Debates over the evolving security environment in the Indo-Pacific have, therefore, naturally developed through the framework of Sino-US relations. Nevertheless, the resurgence and collaboration of these two powers reveal an intricate and profound transformation of the international order. Moreover, the vital role that maritime powers play in the international order makes the rise of these two powers even more consequential.

The strategic partnership between India and Japan deserves more attention, not only as a mere counter to China's aggression but also as a means to maintain and cultivate a robust, open and liberal international order in an uncertain Indo-Pacific through the rise of internationalism in both capitals. The rising tensions in the contested waters of the South China Sea will upset the maritime order in the Indo-Pacific. Gaining supremacy over the South China Sea allows a power to have unparalleled command of the order in the Indo-Pacific. Intensifying tensions in these strategically critical waters, especially for trade and commerce of this vibrant region, therefore, not only exhibit a crisis in the maritime order but also the future of the international order of the region as a whole. The close linkage between the international order and the maritime order makes the rise of these two maritime powers, namely Japan and India, even more consequential.

Japan's proactive foreign policy is also considered as a product of the change in the international security environment in the Asia-Pacific in the past 25 years with a combination of shifts in Tokyo's perception of the world and external pressure (*gaiatsu*) from Washington to enhance Tokyo's role in regional security. In other words, as a leading Japan expert at Washington University, Kenneth Pyle argues, "the foreign policy of modern Japan has been influenced and shaped to an unusually large degree by the international system". [29]

Regarding India, Prime Minister Modi's increasingly proactive foreign policy, assuming more geopolitical role in the Indo-Pacific and viewing military power more as an integral part of foreign policy is an aberration from India's past foreign policy tradition. Nevertheless, it is also a culmination of several significant changes regarding India's international standing that occurred in the past quarter of a century.

In short, all the above analysis narrating the fact that the emerging strategic partnership between Japan and India and the role of Japan in India's 'Act East Policy', is a product of several multilayered factors. First of all, it is clearly informed by a balancing behaviour as the power distribution in the region changes. In addition, it also reflects the two nations' sense of purpose or in other words, internationalism. After the end of the Cold War, both countries searched their role in the international order.

In both countries, the origin of the shift towards a more proactive security policy could be found in the 1990s. While the rise of Japan and India is a strategic reaction towards China's assertiveness, the origins of changes in their security policies imply that it is unhelpful to attribute the policy changes solely to China's behaviour. The engagement of these major powers reveals that the transformation of the security environment in the region exhibits an "order transition" rather than a "power transition". The rise of previously reluctant powers, Japan and India has enormous potential in weathering international political order in the 21st century. It is up to the policymakers in the US, Japan and India to seize this unique opportunity.

Notes and References

1. This is a concept used by Evelyn Goh to explain the geopolitical changes in East Asia. Goh, Evelyn (2013), "The Struggle for Order: Hegemony, Hierarchy, and Transition in Post-Cold War East Asia", Oxford: Oxford University Press.
2. T.R. Sareen (2007), "India and Japan in Historical Perspective", Lecture Series on Japan, Issue No. 4, New Delhi: The Japan Foundation, January, p. 9.
3. Arpitha Mathur (2012), "India-Japan Relations: Drivers, Trends and Prospects", RSIS Monograph No. 23, (Singapore: S. Rajaratnam School of International Studies, p. 5.
4. Ibid., pp. 10-11.
5. When Indians decided to follow the *swadeshi* system of boycotting foreign goods, Japanese goods were excluded from the banned category. In fact, a prominent Indian newspaper *Kesari* clearly called on people to choose Japanese goods over all other foreign manufactured ones. For more details see Birendra Prasad, "Indian Nationalism and Asia, 1900-1947", Delhi: B.R. Publishing Corporation, 1979, pp. 44-45.
6. Rash Bihary Bose who came to be known as the "Bose of Nakamuraya" not only took political asylum in Japan, married a native woman, but also spent his entire life in the country as a Japanese citizen (from 1924) till his death in January 1945.
7. J.N. Dixit (1996), "My South Block Years: Memoirs of a Foreign Secretary", New Delhi: UBSPD, p. 254.
8. Shibashis Chatterjee (2007), "Conceptions of Space in India's Look East Policy: Order, Cooperation or Community?", *South Asian Survey*, Vol. 14, No. 1, p. 72.
9. As cited in David Scott, "India's 'Extended Neighbourhood' Concept: Power Projection for a Rising Power", *India Review*, Vol. 8, No. 2, April-June 2009, p. 125.
10. As cited in Takio Yamada, "Japan-India Relations: A Time for Sea Change", in K. Kesavapany, A. Mani and P. Ramaswamy (eds.), 'Rising India and Indian Communities in East Asia', Singapore: Institute of Southeast Asian Studies, 2008, p. 150.
11. The National Security Strategy of the United States of America, September 2002, available at:

http://merln.ndu.edu/whitepapers/USnss2002.pdf.

12. Swati Arun, "No, India Should Not Seek an Alliance With Japan", available at: http://thediplomat.com/2014/09/no-india-should-not-seek-an-alliance-with-japan.
13. "India-Japan Vision Statement", Ministry of External Affairs, Government of India, October 29, 2018, available at: https://www.mea.gov.in/bilateral-documents.htm?dtl/30543/IndiaJapan_Vision_Statement.
14. K.V. Kesavan, "India and Major Powers: Japan", Raisisna Debates, Observer Research Foundation, August 9, 2019, available at: https://www.orfonline.org/expert-speak/india-and-major-powers-japan-54248.
15. Ibid.
16. Ibid
17. Vikas Dhoot, "An Abe-Modi Plan for Africa", *The Hindu*, May 24, 2017, available at: https://www.thehindu.com/news/national/abe-modi-plan-unveiled/article18572502.ece.
18. S.D. Muni (2011), "India's Look East Policy: The Strategic Dimension", ISAS Working Paper No. 121, February 1, 2011, Institute of South Asian Studies, National University of Singapore, available at: ISAS_Working_Paper_121-_Email-_India's_'Look East'_Policy_The_Strategic_Dimension_01022011145800.pdf, p.?,
19. Press Trust of India, "Time for 'Act East Policy' and Not Just 'Look East': Swaraj", *Business Standard*, New Delhi, August 25, 2014.
20. Danielle Rajendram (2014), "India's New Asia-Pacific Strategy: Modi Acts East", Lowy. Institute for International Policy. December 2014, available at: www.Lowyinstitute.org/, p.4.
21. Miles Kahler (1993), "Multilateralism with Small and Large Numbers" in John Gerard Reggie (ed.), 'Multilateralism Matter: The Theory and Praxis of an Institutional Form', New York: Columbia University Press, pp. 295-326; Thomas Wright (2009), "Towards Effective Multilateralism: Why Bigger May Not Be Better?", *Washington Quarterly*, Vol. 32, No. 4; Moises

Naim (2009), "Minilateralism: The Magic Number to Get Real International Action", *Foreign Policy*, June 22, available at: www.foreignpolicy.com/articles/2009/06/18/minilateralism.
22. Swaran Singh and Lilian Yamamoto (2016), "Quads and Triangles: Locating Japan in India's Act East Policy", *Global Outlook*, Vol. 1, No. 1, Spring, p. 116.
23. Jean-Luc Racine (2015), "From the Grame Game 3.0 to the U.S. Asia Pivot: The New Geometry of South Asia's Geopolitics", in Siegfried O. Wolf et al., 'Politics in South Asia: Culture, Rationality and Conceptual Flow', New York: Springer, p. 148; also see Brig M.N. Sarin (Retd.), "Mending Fences, Cross Infiltration and Conflict Challenges: Line of Actual Control", Delhi: Gaurav Book Centre Pvt. Ltd., p. 16.
24. U.S. Department of Defence (2012), "Sustaining US Global Leadership: Priorities for 21st Century Defence", available at: http://archive.defense.gov/news/Defense_Strategic_Guidance.pdf.
25. C. Fred Bergsten (2015), "India's Rise: Towards Trade-Led Growth", Peterson Institute of International Economics, September, p. 13; also Raghav Bahl (2015), "Super Economies: America, India, China and the Future of the World", Gurgaon: Penguin Books, p. 32.
26. Robert D. Blackwill and Ashley J. Tellis (2015), "Revising U.S. Grand Strategy towards China", Council on Foreign Relations, Council Special Report No. 72, March, p. 30.
27. Takuya Matsuda, "The Rise of Reluctant Powers: The India-Japan Strategic Partnership and the Evolving International Order of the Indo-Pacific", available at: http://web.isanet.org/Web/Conferences/HKU2017-s/Archive/c34e8248-ed9f-4866-b9e3-bed44f525256.pdf.
28. Ibid.
29. Kenneth Pyle (2007), "Japan Rising: The Resurgence of Japanese Power and Purpose", New York: Public Affairs.

Index

Index